LUMINOUS
LANDSCAPE
OF THE
AFTERLIFE

"In *The Luminous Landscape of the Afterlife* we are offered a spirit-inspired glimpse of what may await us beyond this life and how to prepare for it now. Above all, we learn that consciousness is eternal, that love is everything, and that death is not the end but rather a series of new beginnings. A thought-provoking and expansive book about the afterlife that will challenge you, offer comfort, and reconnect you with who and what you are and why you're here."

JOHN P. FORSYTH, PH.D., COAUTHOR OF *THE MINDFULNESS AND ACCEPTANCE WORKBOOK FOR ANXIETY* AND *ANXIETY HAPPENS*

"As someone who works intimately with death, dying, and those on the other side, I am impressed with how this book offers the reader accurate insight of what to expect when the body leaves this human planetary experience and crosses over. Matthew and Jordan give detailed explanations of the Akashic Record, consciousness, and energy, allowing for a love-filled preview of what exists in the afterlife. It is a beautiful guide to open not only the mind but the heart."

SUZANNE WORTHLEY, ENERGY PRACTITIONER, INTUITIVE, AND AUTHOR OF *AN ENERGY HEALER'S BOOK OF DYING*

THE LUMINOUS LANDSCAPE OF THE AFTERLIFE

JORDAN'S MESSAGE TO THE LIVING ON WHAT TO EXPECT AFTER DEATH

A Sacred Planet Book

MATTHEW McKAY, PH.D.

Park Street Press
Rochester, Vermont

Park Street Press
One Park Street
Rochester, Vermont 05767
www.ParkStPress.com

Text stock is SFI certified

Park Street Press is a division of Inner Traditions International

Sacred Planet Books are curated by Richard Grossinger, Inner Traditions editorial board member and cofounder and former publisher of North Atlantic Books. The Sacred Planet collection, published under the umbrella of the Inner Traditions family of imprints, is comprised of works on the themes of consciousness, cosmology, alternative medicine, dreams, climate, permaculture, alchemy, shamanic studies, oracles, astrology, crystals, hyperobjects, locutions, and subtle bodies.

Cataloging-in-Publication Data for this title is available from the Library of Congress

ISBN 978-1-64411-284-7 (print)
ISBN 978-1-64411-285-4 (ebook)

Printed and bound in the United States by Lake Book Manufacturing, Inc. The text stock is SFI certified. The Sustainable Forestry Initiative® program promotes sustainable forest management.

10 9 8 7 6 5 4 3 2

Text design and layout by Virginia Scott Bowman
This book was typeset in Garamond Premier Pro with Gotham Condensed used as the display typeface

To send correspondence to the author of this book, mail a first-class letter to the author c/o Inner Traditions • Bear & Company, One Park Street, Rochester, VT 05767, and we will forward the communication, or contact the author directly at **matt@ newharbinger.com.**

Contents

Jordan's Book of the Dead

Foreword

Suzanne Giesemann

WHEN IS THE LAST TIME you planned a trip to an unfamiliar place? If you're like most people, you probably did a little advance planning. Perhaps you bought a guidebook and a map or two. It's highly likely that you searched the internet for information on the local food, language, geography, and customs. Very few people travel to a new destination without some idea of what awaits them.

Unfortunately, the same cannot be said of the journey across the veil.

Even though no human can avoid the ultimate malfunction of the physical body, death is both an unpopular and uncomfortable topic of conversation. The subject is often avoided at all costs, even if such head-in-the-sand behavior results in emotional discomfort and important decisions left unmade in one's final hours. Consequently, information about the afterlife remains sketchy at best and greatly misconstrued at worst.

The cause of this ignorance is fear of the unknown and reliance on stories passed down about the afterlife that read like one of Grimm's fairy tales. Guidebooks to this shared destination are few and far between. One of the most well-known texts, *The Tibetan Book of the Dead,* is a translation of parts of an eighth-century work. It contains teachings similar to *The Egyptian Book of the Dead,* another one you won't find on any bestseller list in the West.

You are also unlikely to find either of these esoteric texts on the shelves next to Lonely Planet's or Fodor's travel guides, despite the benefits that having a detailed description of the afterlife can provide. Whether this lack of popularity is due to the heavy subject matter or the books' heavy writing style, the next phase of a soul's travels remains for most people a great mystery.

Enter Matthew and Jordan McKay. The information in this clear, concise, modern-day guide to the afterlife was received through the merged minds of father and son through a process known as channeling. Jordan provided the dictation; his father, Matthew, served as the scribe. Those who haven't personally experienced this form of inspired writing may conclude that the content came from Matthew's imagination. We cannot prove otherwise, but I wager that Matthew, an eminent psychologist, could provide quite a convincing argument to the contrary.

Matthew might explain that he could not possibly have conjured up the descriptions shared in these pages. He might assure you that he had never previously envisioned the kind of scenarios described so succinctly by his son. He might take you step by step through the channeling process, as he does in the appendix, so that you might experience channeling for yourself. In the end, you will have to decide if the information Jordan shares through this book is true. Whether you believe what he says is your choice, but happily, your body has a built-in truth meter that helps you discern what information you can trust.

As you read Jordan's words, pay attention to the area around your heart and solar plexus to perform what I call "the heart test." If the information rings true, you will experience a feeling of openness and lightness with no constriction. If the information does not resonate with you, this area will reflexively tighten. In some cases, this reaction will be due to the fear of being asked to change your basic worldview.

There is quite a lot of information in this book that may well challenge cherished beliefs. A wise woman once told me that if our teachers don't make us squirm, they aren't doing their job. In *The Luminous Landscape of the Afterlife*, Jordan takes the role of a teacher, or guide, to the afterlife. His concepts may indeed cause you some discomfort. As this happens, I encourage you to pause and take a few deep breaths. Be willing to entertain the possibility that your beliefs may have been passed down by those who have not had the personal experience that Jordan has.

The first time I experienced words flowing unbidden into my mind as Matthew has, I was sure that I was making them up. It took a year's worth of receiving meaningful messages in the form of perfectly rhyming poems to convince me that the words came from a higher level of consciousness than my own. Gratefully, I surrendered all doubt and fear of ridicule and listened to my heart. I came to appreciate the gift that channeling affords all of us—a window to a love-filled reality that is as close as our breath and ultimately more familiar than our earthly homes.

As a medium who has been tested by respected research scientists, I have had the personal experience of communicating with thousands of souls like Jordan. Thanks to my background as a U.S. Navy commander and commanding officer, nothing less than verifiable evidence provided by these souls and the tangible feeling of their presence would have convinced me these were not the figments of an overactive imagination. The preponderance of the evidence from those who have passed allows me to assure you that this life is not all there is. As Jordan so clearly shows us in this book, death is merely a transition to another chapter in our eternal existence as a soul.

I am well familiar with much of the information about the afterlife that Jordan shares in this book. His words register strongly as truth and align with what my nonphysical guides and others in spirit have unanimously shared with me. Through this fascinating book, Jordan has expanded my understanding with several concepts that I had never heard before, yet each passed "the heart test."

Other than the brief introduction and appendices written by Matthew, all of the words you are about to enjoy are solely Jordan's. This treasure of a book is at times poetic and at times practical and includes guided meditations for you to enjoy and learn from your own experience of expanded awareness.

Our intrepid guide invites you to recall occasions in which you lost yourself in the moment or when you enjoyed an intense sense of belonging. Such mental exercises will entice you with glimpses of your future, but even better, they will show you that you can indeed experience heaven on Earth when you focus on what matters most.

Prepare to take a journey with Jordan to a land that seems at times stunningly similar to the one you now experience yet is far less judgmental and infinitely more loving. The territory described in this new book of the dead may not have changed since the publication date of previous "books of the dead," but humans most certainly have. Modern readers are more open to learning from various sources what awaits us without being told what to believe. We are ready for a version of the afterlife that doesn't require us to be other than what we are: fallible humans who learn by trial and error and who continue learning even after the transition we call death.

As Jordan states, this is the ultimate self-help guide. He shares his deep wisdom not only to assist you in navigating unknown terrain when your time comes to cross the veil but also to support you in understanding and better appreciating the challenges you face now in human form.

Reading these pages, one has the distinct awareness that this is no longer the young man his father knew when Jordan walked in physical form, but an expanded version of Matthew's son. This is Jordan's soul talking to you, and if you listen ever so carefully, you will hear him speaking soul to soul.

SUZANNE GIESEMANN is the author of thirteen books, including *Messages of Hope*. She is the founder of the Awakened Way, a path to knowing who you are and why you're here.

Author's
Introduction

I HAVE LOVED JORDAN for thirty-four years in this life. But for much of that time he has not been here; I haven't been able to hold and kiss him. At age twenty-three, on the way home from work, he was accosted by men who probably wanted to steal his bike. They all fought, and as he was breaking away, Jordan was shot in the back. When my boy died, I had no belief that the dead could talk to us. At best, they seemed gone in another world, separated by loss and the deafening thunder of our grief. Perhaps, even worse, their passing spoke a truth far more dire: that they ceased to exist and that these sweet, ephemeral spirits lived only in memory.

But then Jordan started speaking to me—at first only in dreams—but then through mediums, through a process called induced after-death communication,* and through the gift of channeled writing he told me he was here. He was with me, and he could teach me what he knows about the afterlife. He has given me something I could never have hoped for: a window into the world of spirit, an invitation to listen at the curtain between worlds, and a clear awareness that death is neither an end nor even a loss. It is merely the time when we finally remember who we are and where our home is.

---

*Alan Botkin, *Induced After-Death Communication: A New Therapy for Healing Grief Trauma* (Charlottesville, Va.: Hampton Roads Publishing, 2005).

THE CHANNELING PROCESS

I have grieved deeply for Jordan because I can't touch him, sit in our kitchen to enjoy a long, rambling conversation, or watch his life unfold. His spirit, or the spirit representing him in this book, doesn't take his place and can't speak for the young man as he would have spoken if he had continued to live on this Earth. The voice speaks for a larger entity that was there before Jordan was born, even as it is there after death. Jordan's voice has been added to that being, but the entity is timeless and views the universe and its own existence from that perspective.

The solace I get from my conversations with Jordan comes from the knowledge that the love between us is still a real and active force, and it opens the bigger picture. The things he conveyed as spirit have a larger meaning than the personal relationship between us. A greater spiritual realm has been revealed. It has an eternal wisdom that doesn't depend on the relationship between Jordan and me but instead depends on the soul knowledge that discarnate beings can convey to the living.

That said, there is no direct speech or even a common language between the dead and the living. Meanings pass from Jordan's spiritual field, where he is now, to my spiritual field, where I am now. And then they pass through my brain into written language. Of course, that language is mine, but it isn't mine instead of Jordan's. It is a language generated out of our living relationship. Jordan can only communicate his radically different experience in terms humans would understand, and I can only translate it into terms that *I* understand. Channeling is not art or literature or ethnography, as there are always filters and contamination. And it isn't merely dictation; it is a collaboration and convergent soul-speak.

There is still the question: How do you know these words are really from Jordan and not my own projections or wishful thinking? There are two very different answers to this basic question. The first is: I know Jordan so well that I recognize his voice, the participation of his separate and special ego in language, tone, style, and humor. I also recognize the voice as not my own at the same time that I feel it as Jordan. He is saying things I don't know, or even come close to knowing, in the way Jordan would say them. There is a gut "dead reckoning" to our exchange. In addition, numerous psychics have independently told me about their own communications with Jordan and the book he was writing. Their information matched the text I received.

The second answer is: it isn't Jordan, meaning it isn't only my son who knows himself as Jordan. The voice is a larger soul or spirit being who knows himself as many things, one of them being Jordan. That is the part that's speaking to me, and that part has dimensions that Jordan as I knew him didn't, not because Jordan lacked something, but because he was engaged in living the life of a boy and then a young man in California. The soul speaking to me *includes* Jordan in its own field of identities, lifetimes, and knowledge.

I respect Jordan's integrity as much as I respect and love and miss him, so I wouldn't assign this book to him if I didn't experience the authenticity of his signature. I am simply saying to take this afterlife guide as an expression of our love for each other in continuing to work together on a common project. It is a gift to you so that you may know death as mere punctuation in the eternal life of your soul.

HOW WE BEGAN

Our first conversations via channeled writing took the form of reassurance that Jordan was happy and in a good place. But that quickly changed into deeper explorations of the nature of time, the reasons we incarnate, the purpose of a physical universe, the relationship between individual souls and the Divine, and many other subjects. About five years into our channeled exchanges, Jordan decided we should write a book. Within a few minutes he had outlined all the chapters, and over time he dictated much of what became our first book, *Seeking Jordan*.* Later he conceived and developed with me a set of spiritual practices to help trauma victims find their life purpose and use the concept of Wise Mind for decision-making. This became *The New Happiness*.†

After finishing, Jordan told me that the fear of death and the struggle souls frequently face as they transition can change. Souls need support, knowledge, and reassurance as they contemplate death and what awaits them. Knowledge and preparation, Jordan says, could fundamentally change how we view and experience our transition to the afterlife.

FEAR OF DEATH

I've spent much of my life struggling with the fear of death. I've imagined my life—and my consciousness winking out—like a star burning its last fuel and going dark. I've imagined all that I've loved and all the love inside of me flung into nothingness. Hell is a lot less frightening to me than the empty dark.

Yet for all that fear, I yearned for the truth—whatever it was. I wanted to pierce the mystery of death to see what was on the other side. Most of us—unless we are cocooned in absolute beliefs—want

---

*Matthew McKay, *Seeking Jordan* (Novato, Calif.: New World Library, 2016).
†Matthew McKay and Jeffrey Wood, *The New Happiness* (Oakland, Calif.: New Harbinger Publications, 2019).

this. We want to know what happens when our breath stops, when the body no longer holds us.

The fear of death impacts a soul in two ways.

First, it turns life into a battle of avoidance. Some may avoid the fear of death through a pursuit of pleasure and distraction, or perhaps money, power, or prestige; others may avoid the fear by numbing, drugging, running, denying, embracing myths, or creating something we hope will survive us. I have done them all.

The fear of death also changes our actual experience of death. The fear makes us deaf and blind to what exists in the afterlife. Fear eclipses love and our relationship to all the souls who died before us. Fear can cause us to hallucinate terrifying scenes of judgment or hell and miss what's really present after death.

POSTDEATH NAVIGATION

At the moment of death, we lose our senses, our nervous system, and all that has anchored us to the world. We lose our families and goals in life. We find ourselves in a place where a thought creates visions, where a mere idea projects images that can capture and overwhelm us. The physical world is gone, and for a time we may not be able to hear or recognize the spirits that have come to help us. The love we feel for our soul group and guides may be masked from us.

In this confusion, souls struggle to get their bearings. Some don't yet recognize that they are dead. Some are so attached to the people and things of their past that they cling to the physical plane. Some are filled with emotions—fear, anger, grief, shame, greed— that obscure the life of spirit. Some souls expect an afterlife that doesn't exist, a picture of heaven painted from pulpits and religious training that prevents them from seeing what's there. Some souls expect nothing, an extinction of consciousness, and can't understand why they are still thinking and aware *outside* of their bodies.

The time immediately after death is disorienting. This is because a soul who has newly crossed over is still an amnesiac. They don't know what they know. How we communicate and navigate in spirit has been forgotten. How to focus our energy in spirit has temporarily been lost. All that we have learned in past lives remains a vague dream. For example, we "see" in all directions. We move by intention rather than physically walking. We "hear" telepathically rather than listening to sound and words. We connect through the medium of love rather than touching or holding or conversing.

At this moment, having been separated from our body, we need to remember who we are, where we are going, and how to get there. That is one purpose of this book. It is a navigational guide to death and the afterlife. It is a resource so you will know what to expect, how to prepare, and what to do as you move through the primary early phases of life after death.

LIFE PURPOSE

Each incarnation to Earth likewise induces a forgetting of all that has gone before. We forget so we can learn the lessons we came here to encounter in this incarnation. We forget so we can take this place seriously, struggling to love in the face of pain and loss and hurt.

Each soul, at each incarnation, enters a body, a family, a social context, and a moment in history destined to teach important lessons. We are let loose there. What and how much we learn is up to us; it depends on the choices we make each day and over all the years of our life.

Learning why you are here and why you entered this body is another reason for this book. Death cannot be understood unless the purpose of life is also recognized. We are not here to be redeemed, proven worthy, or to earn a high station in heaven. We are here, Jordan says, to love and to learn. Death merely facilitates moving from the physical dimensions into the world of spirit. Our life as a soul has the same goals—here and in the afterlife—to evolve and to grow.

CREATING A NEW BOOK
OF THE DEAD

Our amnesia—forgetting why we are here and what happens in the afterlife—can be broken in many ways. There are meditations that can pierce the veil, or there are drugs, trance states, deprivations (food, sleep, oxygen), and cultivated forms of pain. The Egyptian and Tibetan Books of the Dead, the Upanishads, and so many mystical and sacred texts have grown from such altered states. The visions in these ancient texts were driven by the experiences and sometimes the needs of the dreamer. Demons, figures of judgment, and evil spirits show up in this literature because such images tap into the root fears of every human. But these images of hell, devils, and malicious spirits don't represent any spiritual reality. They are merely human projections, and Jordan seeks to explain these visions and correct such misperceptions in the book you are now reading.

Jordan channeled this book to offer four things every soul needs:

+ to know why we're here
+ to know what to expect at death and transition
+ to know how to navigate without a body
+ to know our work in the spirit world

Jordan has died many times, gone to the afterlife, and returned here to live in another place and time and body. He remembers all of it. This is his story and the fruit of all that he has learned.

Jordan's
Book of the Dead

CHAPTER 1

My Death and Transition

I FELT COLD, ODDLY, EVEN THOUGH I was out of my body. And a sense of shock. I had been knocking on a door. I thought I had lost consciousness and come to again. But I wasn't quite in my body—I was a little above it. My body was slumped below. I was examining myself to see what was wrong but couldn't figure out why I was outside my body.

I couldn't seem to move. I willed my arm to move, to pull upright. Nothing happened. And now I started to get alarmed. Not a physical anxiety where you feel the adrenaline coursing through you, but a sense that something wasn't right, and maybe never would be again as far as Jordan was concerned. It was a sense of severe disturbance. My body just lay there, and I started to notice I felt detached from it. I was a little farther above it when someone opened the door and looked at me. Again, I tried to move, but I was starting to understand that I couldn't.

There were voices. A car went by on the street. The men who had shot me had already left. I started to feel like it wasn't important, whatever was going on. And that, too, alarmed me. I had just been in the fight of my life, and I had been desperate for help, and now it seemed to have lost importance. The street, the houses, the people in the houses seemed without great significance as I looked around.

I was floating higher. I knew that wasn't right. Nothing had ever happened like this in my life as Jordan. It occurred to me that I was dead, and that struck me with horror. Not so much for myself, but for everyone I loved, all that I was connected to. I was on my way home to Elisa—I was so sad at the thought that I couldn't reach her or talk to her. The sadness continued as I thought about my mom and dad, my sisters, my friends. I was gone, this hovering ghost, out of their lives. The panic of disconnection, for me, was intense.

Maybe it was because I was young, so fully *in* my life, so fully *expecting* to live, that this shock of loss stayed with me. I thought of the route to the flat I shared with Elisa and found myself covering that ground very quickly, almost instantly. I simply went through the wall to our bedroom and watched her sleep. I would never hold or talk to her again. It was a feeling not of tears, but a sense of time stretching out without each other, a bleakness.

In this state, I visited my friend Mauchi. He immediately awoke, feeling a deep disturbance in the room that he interpreted as evil. I visited my sleeping parents, more careful now not to disturb them. When I thought of someone and pictured where they were, I could be there. But if I couldn't visualize their location, I seemed blocked to get to them.

Now I can be with anyone I want instantly just by thinking of them. But then, in the first hours after my death, I could only go to places I knew well. All this "visiting," by the way, happened while I still seemed anchored to that street. I would think of and see someone I loved, but I still—at the same time—seemed to remain near my body.

Paramedics came. They rolled me over, pulled open my clothes, and examined me. Somehow this strengthened my awareness that Jordan was gone; he was dead. That body, so familiar, so "me," wasn't me anymore. With great sadness I could feel a severing, a letting go of my attachment to Jordan as a physical being. And as this happened things just got gray. It wasn't like I was going anywhere—up to some heaven, or into a tunnel—but my surroundings just faded and disappeared. I think I no longer wanted to be there, to see my body touched and moved and prodded, to see people standing around me—talking or reacting in whatever way. I just didn't want to see it, so the physical elements of the scene dissolved.

REACHING THE LANDING PLACE

I didn't know where I was, and that held its own alarm. I could hear something like wind, but it was probably more like breath. I was moving, but with no sense of direction. Just away. While I still had a sense of arms and legs, I held them close. My energy was very compact.

At some point, there was more light—as if the morning sun were just starting to penetrate a mist. In fact, I thought perhaps the sun was coming up. I died at night, and I had a strange moment of relief that day was dawning. Another day! Life, or some form of it. But the light ultimately became brighter than any dawn, and shapes—tall, vertical shadows—began to appear in the mist. There was a sense of ground, although I wasn't actually standing on anything. The shadows clarified, and I saw that they were souls—my father and mother, my sisters—but I couldn't figure out how they could be here because they weren't dead.

My soul knowledge—the awareness of all I've learned in my lives and in the spirit world—still wasn't available to me. I thought of the home where I grew up in Berkeley, and it appeared. I thought of Barrett's* house, and I could see that. I thought of my job, and I could see my computer and desk and all that was on it. There was a jumble of stuff around me, remnants of Jordan's life that seemed real. But they were just images made of energy. I was projecting. All this was happening lightning fast, and I could feel a hand touching me, urging me to slow down. I received the information telepathically. I could also feel love bathing me, radiating from the souls around me, but also from the light itself.

Someone, a guide perhaps, asked me to select one image that could stabilize the scene. Some place beautiful or peaceful that I liked. I was told we could use it like a stage backdrop so I could settle down here. I chose a meadow in Yosemite. As I thought about it, the Berkeley house and the rest of the clutter started to disappear. I could fill in the scene almost like I was painting a watercolor super fast— and now I was in this beautiful meadow with my mom and dad and sisters and some other souls farther off but coming toward me.

I wasn't sure what I was making up and what was real. I imagined an elephant in Yosemite, and there it was. I thought up a sci-fi monster, and it was right next to the elephant. The monster and the elephant started fighting, stomping around.

---

*A dear family friend

I could feel the ground shake. It was out of hand and scary because if I wasn't careful, anything I conjured in my mind would show up in the meadow. I didn't know how to manage it. Things were appearing and disappearing, depending on what I gave my attention to. I thought of Yosemite Falls, and I could hear the rifle crack and thunder of the plummeting water.

I had no idea how to control this. My family was there but fading in and out as I struggled to manage the scene. After a while, and with help I think, I started to realize it's like learning to coordinate the knobs on an Etch A Sketch. One knob is your attention, and one knob is intention. If all you turn is the attention knob, you'll see whatever you think about. The *intention* knob is what you want to see or create. Intention won't work without clear attention; and vice versa.

It seemed like a good while before I got used to the way thought creates energetic and vibrational shifts that, in turn, create images. I found myself doing (or encouraged to do) a form of meditation where you anchor your focus on one thing to calm the frenetic shifting and morphing of images. It seemed like the thing I focused on was a sound, but really it was love—a deep sense of love communicated from the beings around me. I listened and held on to this. The stream of love contained knowledge not in the form of words, but as whole concepts, a complex understanding. Through this medium, I was told that I was in a landing place. It was just outside, or adjacent to, the spirit world. I would remain here until my residual distress from my death, or emotional tailings from my last life, had calmed. In this place, I was also adjusting to a bodiless state—no limbic or nervous system, no strong cravings or desire, no physical experience of movement. The love stream communicated that I was safe, protected. All I had to do was listen. The sound of love is like the murmur of a thousand low-pitched voices, and with it is a sense of belonging, of being part of a great whole. I belong not just with the souls of my family, but to a sense of all, of *all that is.*

As the meadow stabilized, and I felt more and more surrounded by this murmur of love, I relaxed. I realized that I had held my soul energy tightly, protectively since my death. As my energy expanded, my vibrational level increased, and I could hear more and more the sound of *all.* Tuning in to this sound, I realized, was the main work I was doing in this landing place. When the sound and feeling of deep connection reached a certain criterion level, I was told a portal would open and I'd be allowed to move into the sanctum of the spirit world.

ENTERING THE SPIRIT WORLD

When you leave the landing place, you leave all possibility of evil, of self-created monsters, of danger. You leave the last traces and manifestations of the physical. You retain the shape of your human body, but you have let go of attachment to it. You are not lingering, a ghost with one foot back on Earth. You are released to be fully spirit, connected to *all.* As such, your soul memories—past lives and your life between lives in the spirit world—start to come back to you. You become, at that moment, fully yourself.

The first thing I remember was trying to survive on the streets of a medieval city. I was begging and alone, and my sole preoccupation was figuring out how to eat and make it to the next day. Then came the flood of other lives: each body I was given was anchored in a particular time and situation and arranged around a particular problem or lesson. I could see them all stretching across time, and I felt the sadness and pain of each life as well as the moments where I gave love.

And then I could see the trajectory of my spiritual learning. I am a fighter for lost causes. In different lives, I have demanded to be heard. I have yearned for truth no one saw, no one believed in. I have given in to defeat as well. I have collapsed. I have been venial in the quest to avoid pain. In the spirit world, I have been learning to put my finger on the exact point in time where change is possible, to see the one event—in the matrix of cause and effect—where history (on whatever scale) shifts and takes a different course.

I could suddenly see all this—both my incarnations and my learning in spirit—as one experience. As the work of one soul that would be given to *all*, to the whole of consciousness. I could see my purpose. I could see the light and hear the sound of love around me.

THE PLACE OF LIFE REVIEW

I felt that all this was familiar ground, and in that was a sense of peace. But now I was moving again, drawn in a direction that emanated the color green. Not the green of plants or living things, but the green of reverie. Of concentration on a task. All around, souls were huddled, focusing inward. I was guided to a spot by a lamppost and lantern where I could meditate on the life just lived. I sat down in a declivity that seemed to mold itself to me and was instructed that I would remain here for the review of Jordan's life. The lantern turned on.

It began with the helplessness of the infant and the bond with my mother. I could feel her inside, how every smile or cry would affect her. I could feel the daily sway of our relationship—from the deep gazing and connection to the moment of breaking when I was in pain and all connection seemed gone. In this oscillation, I learned about the unconquerable cycle of love and loss that marks our lives on Earth. I felt the timelessness of love, that a moment between mother and son carried the light of all the love in the universe.

I moved forward—to my relationship with my sister Bekah. I relived each cruelty I inflicted on her. Over and over, moment after moment of my anger. I felt it not as I experienced it, but as she hurt and took in the pain on the other side.

While I was contemplating the way I'd hurt her, I knew I could get up at any time and stop the review. But I didn't want to. Despite the pain of witnessing hurt I'd caused, I wanted to learn. I felt a deep need to know how my actions had affected her. While the review was mostly chronological, it periodically skipped ahead—years later—to related moments with Bekah. But these balancing moments were times of kindness or connection, and I could see her feeling soothed or the way little expressions of love filled her. The rapid contrast of the impacts of cruelty and kindness affected me greatly. I could see the devastating effects of one and the joyous response to the other *in the same soul.* This lesson burned a deep impression on me that I carry now, in my current incarnation.

The effects of my actions toward my succession of girlfriends came next. I learned that truly seeing and hearing them was what helped them most, not all my advice and suggestions. And what hurt them most was withdrawal and disdain. Critical words did far less harm than pulling away. Withdrawing love, I began to see, is on the continuum with hate, a form of disconnection that separates souls and makes every kind of cruelty possible.

I saw my struggles with my mother in the same light— how withdrawal and *not seeing* begets cruelty. When I finally saw her, after I went to college, my anger disappeared. All I had was love.

Periodically, during my time in life review, guides would come to deliberately break the contemplation. I would rest and get an energy bath that was healing. I would telepathically share with them what I was learning—trying to put it together and make sense of what I saw. There is great beauty in seeing the truth, knowing finally the laws of relationship that I sensed only dimly in my life as Jordan.

The laws of relationship are nothing more than recognizing the specific behaviors that express and deepen love. Behaviors that disconnect souls, diminishing the energy that joins them, ultimately lead to every evil we experience on Earth. I was seeing this, and even though I had found these same lessons after previous lives, the lessons seemed new and vitally important to me.

NO JUDGMENTS

There is no judgment in the afterlife. Everything I learned during the review, even when painful, was in an atmosphere of acceptance. When I saw things I did that were not effective, wise, or aligned with love, I didn't experience myself as bad or defective. I was just a soul learning—and sometimes failing to learn—difficult lessons.

In the afterlife, we see things with love. With love we recognize what has been achieved in a particular soul's development and what is missing. In the spirit world, where there is no hurt or yearning, it's easy to see, without judgment, what's missing and what has not been learned. When we are incarnate, the pain of loss and desire drives judgment. In the afterlife, we observe ourselves and every other soul *as that soul is* with absolute acceptance.

THE LITTLE CELEBRATIONS

There were many moments in my life as Jordan that I was glad to relive. I learned a lot about tenacity, about committing to goals and pushing through obstacles. More and more I seemed to have the courage to face difficult situations and emotions. I saw that I often chose to be kind. And in the last year of my life, I learned a lot about expressing my true feelings and needs, about how to give and take in a relationship. My life seemed increasingly guided by love. These moments, as I watched them, brought a surge of well-being. I wasn't so much proud of myself or taking some kind of credit as I was content, held in a small, warm wave of comfort and celebration.

DOWN ON THE FARM

When I finished Jordan's life review, a guide turned out the lamp that hung above my place of recollection. I was led to a passageway—a wide hallway, perhaps more like a tube—of light. Other passageways branched out at intervals as I began to move, but they didn't feel familiar. I knew I was heading for home, and my energy was so intense, it felt like it was splashing over the brim. Hallways leading to city-size collections of soul families flashed by, and sometimes I had brief curiosity about where they led.

A passageway to my left, appearing exactly like the others, nonetheless had a familiar energy pattern. It was like a place on Earth that has a familiar, unmistakable smell. I turned. Now there were other souls going in the opposite direction. I knew I was close to home.

If you think of each soul as a point of light, the spirit world is a vast array of such lights. It has far more lights than the population of Earth because souls reincarnate to many other planets and dimensions. And there are souls who have never incarnated, souls who have completed their incarnations, and souls who cluster to create, who are the source, who turn knowledge into energy and matter. You might think of the spirit world as a gigantic brain, with each cell (soul) located in a particular place and performing a particular function. This brain contains all of consciousness, all of thought, all that has been learned, all creativity, and all love. This brain—the spirit world—is collective consciousness, *all that is.*

I was now heading back to my region—my town and my family. And as I drew closer, the familiar energy and vibrational patterns were like the rooflines and storefronts on Main Street of one's hometown. I turned at one branch and then another, the unique vibrations like street signs or particular notes on an infinite scale.

My soul group, "the farm," appears to live in an old Victorian house. This isn't a physical house, but energy we project—by agreement—to resemble a house. We didn't always use this image to denote our home—we projected caves and reed huts and buildings made of stone. We create the image that is comforting to us—much the same as souls who incarnate as water creatures might project a quiet lake or bay. We call our soul group "the farm" because we are working to learn methods for helping consciousness grow on a mass level. It sounds grandiose, but it just amounts to identifying small, initial steps that can have a large ripple effect. The laws of change are a part of what we study.

They were all waiting for me, just outside the door, appearing as they looked in our most recent shared life. Eleven of them, and I make twelve. There was also a scattering of souls from nearby families—souls with whom I've experienced significant lives.

Each caressed me with a particular expression of love. Though my incarnation was expected to be short, I was held in a kind of group embrace to soothe the sudden loss of my life as Jordan. They were telling me it was a good life. A life well-lived. Each soul, each with a signature and unique energy, looked at me, saw the true nature of who I am, and offered a love that can only come from such knowledge. All the loneliness of my life on Earth was suddenly gone. Elisa, with whom I've mated in many lives and my partner in the last year of Jordan's life, gave me a sort of kiss. Her energy entered me like a drug entering a physical body. Though Elisa was still incarnate, as were other souls in my group, some of their energy remained behind. Our Victorian held some essence of them in much the same way our bedrooms on Earth hold our most precious possessions while we're away.

I was home. But all that I had loved and learned as Jordan was still alive in me.

CHAPTER 2

Landing at the Gate

THE LANDING PLACE lies at the gateway to the world of spirit. It's not an actual location, like on a map, but an energy field reserved for calming and instructing incoming souls—like orientation when you go to college, but in this case the focus is on adjusting to being discarnate. While you often still have the residual shape of a body, it is made of energy vibrations, not matter, so you have no sensory or nervous system, no functional limbs.

The problem is *projection*. In spirit, whatever you think or feel or believe can show up as very real-looking images. Remember my experience seeing everything I thought about—elephants, waterfalls, monsters? That's typical. Souls can get stuck for periods of time in bardos; they think they are still on Earth, and hallucinate their house, work setting, and friends. They can make up whole dreamlike scenarios with elaborate plots, dramatic crises, and surges of intense emotions.

Souls who don't know they're dead or who have no belief in the afterlife often stay in these bardos until guides can enter their energy patterns and drop in new suggested images and thoughts. It's like trying to wake someone from a deep sleep—nudging and pushing and whispering, and finally shouting and rocking them. The guides are required to make more and more forceful interventions until these confused souls begin awakening to their life in spirit.

THE HEALING PLACE

Souls who remain confused, whose hallucinations block seeing the peaceful landing place that was prepared for them, are taken to a place of healing, where they are treated with more powerful techniques. The healing place is also an intake center for souls who've been greatly damaged by their last life and carry emotions—particularly despair, fear, anger, shame, and greed—that cannot enter the spirit world. They skip the landing place and go directly to be healed. These souls need intensive care—work to repair and remodel their energy. Memories from past lives, their soul groups, and life between lives are introduced, almost like medicine in an IV drip. At first, these memories are woven into their hallucinated story line, but they gradually blend together to re-establish the soul's history. More on the healing place later.

HOW TO COPE WITH LANDING

The biggest problem when you land isn't your thought-generated images. Your biggest problem is *not* listening. In the landing place, you are surrounded by a unique vibrational pattern that can be described as love. But it extends beyond the meaning of that word on Earth. It means being known and cherished at the same time, and it is also the experience of complete belonging, of being one. Souls experience this vibration in the way they can best receive it. If your body on Earth was most sensitive to auditory experiences, you're likely—as I did—to experience love as a sound. If you were more visual, it could be taken in as light or vibrant color. If you were oriented to sensations of touch, you might feel bathed in warmth.

However the vibration hits you, you've got to be alert and "listen" for love and belonging. If you miss it, you are deaf in the spirit world because all specific communication comes through this medium. Just as voices on Earth are transmitted by vibrating air molecules, so are the telepathic "words" of guides carried in this vibrational level. Let me push the analogy further: on Earth, air (what we breathe and speak through) has exactly the same function as love in the spirit world; it surrounds us, it is the source of spiritual life, and we communicate through love.

So listening for love is the first and foremost task of an arriving soul. That's why souls whose lives were marked by greed or anger are DOA—deaf on arrival—and must go immediately to the healing place. If you're hallucinating wild, uncontrollable images—as I was—direct your attention to the experience of love, be it through sound, light, or touch. In the way a dog will suddenly become still and turn his ears in all directions at some faint sound, you must try to listen, see, or feel for love in all directions. Be still. Try to empty your mind of thoughts (because they become Technicolor images), and open to that feeling of being home, of being cherished. There's a meditation at the end of the chapter to prepare for this.

Once you begin to hear love, the guides can speak to you.

Your loved ones, who've come to greet you, can shower you with joy and affection. It's a moment of great beauty when the amnesia of incarnate life lifts and you know you're back home.

It's often the case that tuning in to the vibrational pattern of love isn't a simple light switch. For a while, you may swing back and forth—from listening to having wild, fearful thoughts and hallucinating everything you imagine. Because anything you think can suddenly surround you, here again, stilling your mind is of the utmost importance. You don't have a breath to focus on in the afterlife, so classic, breath-centered meditations don't work. But you can hear and you can see, so you need to focus on what's there: on a guide or loved one, if you can clearly see them, or on the vibration of belonging, of being one, however it shows up. Keep your attention on one of these, just as you would your breath when meditating on Earth.

Whenever a thought arises, threatening to tear your attention away, refocus on love or one of the souls supporting you. Should a thought or image blossom into a full hallucination, remember that you are just making this up. And no matter how real or intricate, what you're seeing is a mere product of your own thought. As soon as possible, re-anchor your attention on love, your guide, or the souls who've greeted you.

If a hallucination captures you, tearing you from the awareness of love, try to watch it as a movie—curious but detached. Observe, but don't get involved in it. If you don't react strongly to the movie, it will fade out, leaving you to see your guide and hear the love that surrounds you. You may go through this process several times, but if you keep stilling and refocusing your mind (you still have a mind, even without your brain), your surroundings will gradually calm down.

Having strong beliefs that run counter to actual experience in the afterlife can create problems on landing. When souls expect to see Jesus, guides arrange for them to see Jesus. When souls expect angels, they are shown angels. When souls expect thunder claps and a sonorous voice of judgment, something like that can be provided—until they begin to hear love and see what's really there. But some beliefs are so rigid that souls remain delusional. This may be because they expect no afterlife or because they expect a life after death immensely different from what the spirit world actually is. Nearly every religion offers images of a particular afterlife. Most of them are far from the truth. Judgment doesn't happen, hell doesn't happen, getting a mansion in the clouds doesn't happen, being in a pantheon of happy warriors doesn't happen, staring at God all day doesn't happen, and living just like you did on Earth (but a little differently) is way off. The Egyptian idea that if you were a peasant on Earth, you'll till fields in heaven is nonsense.

These beliefs can be challenging to surrender, but more difficult yet are rigid beliefs about right and wrong. Some souls arrive in the afterlife thinking they were bad or evil, and they expect to be sent to hell. Conversely, there are souls who believe they've lived unblemished lives and expect some kingly reward. They are dismayed when nothing of the like is forthcoming and learn, during their life review, that they've failed at some important lessons.

What's right is love and oneness, and what is wrong is disconnection. This isn't moral right or wrong. It is the core spiritual truth. Many souls arrive with a set of religious or moral values that are at odds with this. It is a painful surprise that may require time in the healing place.

It's important to prepare during life for a possible discontinuity between what you *believe* about right and wrong and life after death and what you may find in the spirit world. Try to develop a sense of humility, of not knowing. Of course, you have beliefs that you need to navigate in the world and make choices. But hold them lightly (all except that you're an immortal soul and surrounded by love), especially as you approach death. Things will be different than you think. Going to the afterlife is like visiting another country with different customs, rules, language, and architecture. Prepare for death in the same way you get ready to travel.

In summary, because love rules the spirit world, to the extent our beliefs and emotions get in the way of love, we may need more time to adjust on landing or special help to heal (see chapter 3). Eventually, when we arrive at a pure moment where love is breath, where love is all that there is, we go through the gate.

We suggest recording the following meditation, with pauses where indicated, and listening daily. The meditation helps you:

+ Accept thoughts as mere products of your mind—they are not real.
+ Notice and accept emotions as temporary experiences

that don't define who you are. The emotions are not you.

✦ Listen to the love that surrounds you.

To begin, select a talisman, an object that connects you in some way to the feeling of love. It should be something relatively small that you can either touch or stare at. It could be something that represents or belonged to a loved one on the other side. It could symbolize God or infinity or a higher power or the *love of all that is*. Choose the object now, and use it whenever you do the meditation.

Meditation to Prepare for the Landing Place

- Touch or look at your talisman. . . .
- Notice your breath. . . . Say to yourself "in" as you inhale and "out" as you exhale. . . .
- Continue to watch your breath, keeping your attention there as much as possible . . . (long pause).
- Now and then, briefly check your thoughts. . . . Notice, whatever they are, that they exist in your mind. They are not real in the world. . . . Acknowledge whatever you're thinking as a thought. "There's a thought," you can say to yourself. . . .
- After briefly noticing your thoughts, return to your breath. . . . Go back and forth: thoughts—breath—thoughts—breath. . . . Accept the thoughts as something your mind needs to do, and then just let go of them. . . . Return to your breath. . . .

- Now become aware of your feelings. Notice any emotion you have right now. Just observe it. . . . It may feel strong or not so strong. After a while, it will change. . . . After a while, when you come back to it, your emotion may already be a little different. . . .
- Go back to your breath. In and out. . . .
- Notice your thoughts; they are in your mind and not in the world. . . .
- Notice your feelings. . . .
- Watch the in and out of your breath . . . your thoughts . . . your feelings . . . your breath. In and out. . . .
- Again, be aware of your talisman, your connection to love. Bring love into awareness—of a soul or God or *all that is*. . . . Hold the love as best you can. . . . Listen to the love as you would sound . . . or picture it . . . or feel it in your body. . . . Feel you are part of the love, one with it. . . . Feel it connect you to *all*. . . . Let yourself expand to be love, to be part of *all*.

CHAPTER 3

The Bardos

FOR MANY SOULS death doesn't begin a nonstop flight to the spirit world. Instead it can start an extended period of confusion and uncertainty. Here are some of the potential layovers that may interrupt our journey back to spirit. The first of these has to do with souls who get stuck on Earth.

Holding On to the Physical Plane

✦ Many souls are afraid to leave the site of their death. They anxiously watch over the body, hoping somehow to reunite with it. In some cases, they may not fully realize they are dead. Or, knowing they're discarnate, they fear leaving the physical world and stay with their remains because it's the only anchor they know to the material universe. They watch with great distress as the doctors cease all ministrations, as orderlies or paramedics wrap and move the body. They wait and watch, often feeling a loss of their identity, their sole link to the familiar life.

This distress can make it hard to feel the tug to leave. As the body cools and is no longer animated by a soul within, they continue to cling. The gentle pull toward spirit is lost, for a time, in a kind of soul panic; the release, the sudden freedom from the physical seems so strange and unfamiliar that the spirit is flooded with an urge to get back "inside."

+ Feelings of loss or incompleteness may also keep souls stuck in the scene. They'll often experience fascination with the drama as it plays out, watching what happens with loved ones, antagonists, or other participants in the death scenario. Strangely, this obsession with the place and circumstances of one's own death can be comforting for some souls. They retain a feeling of connection to the actors in the play that's just completed. They are calmed by proximity to the energy and emotions that linger—often for quite a while—at the scene of one's own death.

Like the frightened souls who continue clinging to their bodies, these souls, who are captured by the emotions of a just past life, can't feel the tug to spirit. They become, for a time, disembodied specters who haunt a place. They are what people call ghosts.

+ It's quite common for souls to feel distress at leaving loved ones. They may stay awhile, trying to visit and give comfort. For a time, I kept entering the rooms of family and friends. I acutely felt the separation and couldn't bear to leave them. Despite being aware of the tug toward spirit, I ignored it, and for many hours I remained a ghost. While I had no interest in my body, or trying to somehow reunite with it, I ached in some way to touch everyone I loved. Those hours, just at the end of my life as Jordan, are among the most painful I've known.

Despite how much I tried, I remained largely helpless to reach and comfort my people.

What makes reaching loved ones still tied to the physical plane more difficult is their low vibration. Souls in the spirit world have a much higher vibrational level than incarnated souls or souls who've just left their bodies. As I rushed from room to room while my loved ones slept, I still hadn't been reunited with my soul knowledge (all I've learned in past lives and between lives) or my connection to *all*. So I lacked much of the power and many of the abilities I have when I'm fully immersed in the spirit world.

THE HEALING PLACE

The healing place is the first stop for many distressed souls. It is quiet, insulated from telepathic and psychic noise. From the outside, it has the appearance of some kind of open-air hospital, with countless souls lying motionless, apparently sleeping. Healing guides minister to them as the souls "live" whatever vivid stories they've created. For some souls these stories are experienced in mental or dream states. Some souls have more serious problems to work out and actually travel to dimensions designed for intensive learning. More on this later.

Once you are assigned to the healing place, you have very little control over events. You are spiritually unconscious. The flow of your stories, the strength of your leftover beliefs and assumptions, and the surges of raw emotion will gradually subside. The treatment process is titrated by guides; you are entirely in their hands.

Souls arrive in the healing place for many reasons. These can include:

+ Dying while in a coma and unaware of the transition.
+ Dying in a psychotic state with a loose grasp of conventional reality and arriving in the spirit world influenced by brain-based hallucinations.
+ Dying a sudden or violent death—in a state of terror or rage—and in some cases not yet knowing they're discarnate.
+ Having had a life strongly influenced by fear and fear avoidance. These souls often arrive terrified, with minds practiced at inventing catastrophic possibilities. Each catastrophic thought turns into a vivid experience that only terrifies them more. The harsh bardos described in the Egyptian and Tibetan Books of the Dead derive from these fear-fueled stories.

  Fear avoidance is also a factor. These souls become frantic, trying to escape the images of their own making. This painful scenario—panicking, trying to get away, and panicking even more when there's nowhere to go— continues until these stories and images are slowly turned around by guides. The best preparation for this bardo, while still incarnate, is to work on the realization that your thoughts aren't real, and use meditation to *observe* thoughts rather than get caught and consumed in them.
+ Having had a life strongly influenced by anger. Anger and violence block the experience of love. Incarnate souls who've learned to respond to pain with anger are unprepared for the spirit world.

Violence is even more problematic. Violence inflicts wounds as much on the perpetrator as the victim. It creates pockets of inert or distorted energy in the perpetrating souls. A part of the soul literally goes dead and loses all responsiveness. These souls, as a result, suffer isolation and cannot hear love. They arrive deeply alone and require major energy transfusions (much like blood transfusions) before they can even begin to connect. Some of them remain in the healing wards for Earth centuries.

✦ Having had a life influenced by greed. Because greed is the product of delusion—that we are all separate, unconnected by love—it leaves souls profoundly confused immediately after death. Their lives have been about having and taking rather than loving and sharing. As with anger, greed isolates; souls see themselves alone, fighting for limited resources. And like angry souls, they arrive largely deaf to love.

✦ Having had a life ending in despair. Souls who despair have missed the point of life. They think life is about achieving happiness and that pain indicates a blatant failure. But life isn't about being happy. It's about learning to love, no matter what level of pain or suffering we face. The pain is an essential part of the lesson, not a sign of failure.

Despair is really the inability to express and act on love during periods of extended pain. When despairing souls—particularly those whose death was a suicide—arrive in the afterlife, they may be unattuned to love. While souls aren't blamed or judged for their despair, it takes time to awaken.

✦ Having had a life marked by shame and self-hate. Shame

occurs when a soul believes their life choices to be at odds with what is good and right. They feel judged, a failure in the eyes of others. Because they believe they are undeserving, they remain deaf to the sound of love permeating the afterlife.

THE STRANGE DIMENSIONS

Souls who go to the healing place, while from outward appearances sleeping, can be elsewhere. Souls with intense, dominant emotional states may have some of their soul energy sent to dimensional realities (special bardos) designed for their recovery. There are dimensions, for example, where matter can appear and disappear by mere intention. The soul, while occupying a physical body, doesn't have to contend with the organ and biochemical systems of the bodies we have on Earth—and that body can't be damaged, no matter what the soul does or conjures up.

In these dimensions, the soul's unprocessed emotions from Earth are turned into adversaries, love objects, events (storms, quakes, arrivals, and departures), familiar environments, alien environments, and elaborate plots with spine-tingling crises and crescendos. The soul conjures most of this, but some elements are added or remodeled by guides to help resolve the jagged remnants of emotions from the soul's last life.

In these and other worlds, the soul's "body" and energy suffer no further damage. A thug or gunman, for example, conjured to represent a soul's paranoia and fear, cannot inflict actual pain or injury. The gun may "fire" but there are no wounds other than a moment of terror.

Souls learn to face and resolve emotional pain in these environments. Those dealing with guilt and shame often conjure accusers and hear whispered disapproval. Souls dealing with anger may create Kafkaesque bardos of injustice and victimization. Souls who are steeped in fear project their own demons in almost the same way 3-D printing works on Earth—and then run or learn to battle with them. Souls struggling with desire and avarice keep acquiring and then losing the things they acquired. Some have confused these bardos with hell, but there is no punishment. These are simply well-designed, concentrated learning environments. These plots function like dreams do on Earth, helping to process pain and distress. And, like dreams, nothing truly bad can happen to souls in the strange dimensions. Guides add small twists to the plots so they can gradually resolve, and the soul's vibrational energy will eventually move to a higher level.

On Earth, strong emotions seem highly charged. But in actuality, souls with residual high emotions have *low* vibrational levels. At these levels, they would be deaf and isolated in the spirit world. They would bounce frantically from one conjured image to another, hallucinating whatever scenes their emotions might induce. This is the spiritual equivalent of being "crazy," and that is why we can't allow souls still struggling with intense emotions into the spirit world.

RESIDUALS OF EVIL

Souls whose response to life has been to cause harm, those who have inflicted great suffering on others, arrive in the afterlife suffering a form of solitary confinement.

To hear love, to feel how it permeates the spirit world, would require a reversal and repudiation of everything they've been. They would have to become aware of how their life diverged from the path of love. Such awareness and contrition is rare in the period immediately following death, so they remain alone for a time. They don't see the guides who minister to them. Their energy, across many areas of their soul "body," is inert. Deadened.

They have become spiritually sclerotic, hardened by the damage they've caused. On Earth, this hardness is adaptive; it is the decommissioning of inherent love and compassion so they don't have to feel the harm they inflict. In the afterlife, it has the effect of causing them to lose their senses so they are, for a while, unreachable.

Some of these souls are stuck in darkness; some struggle in dimensions where they feel (emotionally but not physically) the pain from every wound they inflict; some are like Robinson Crusoe, living alone in bardos where every day is the same with nothing they can do to change it.

As these souls slowly awaken to love, as their hardened energy is restored, they must encounter a yet more difficult fate: life review. Though guides are compassionate and without judgment, the process is a merciless truth telling. These souls must experience every moment of pain they've caused. They must feel a depth of regret that a human body couldn't contain, that would be disintegrating on Earth. Nevertheless, most souls choose to face this.

Souls who can't face life review remain in the anterooms of the spirit world. They are not in hell; they are not punished. They yearn for love and connection, but cannot have it. They hunger for their soul group, their familiar guides, but they have no passport. They no longer belong to *all;* they are no longer citizens of spirit.

EVIL FROM GOOD INTENTIONS

Some souls cause great pain out of the intention for good. On Earth, they live under a belief system that justifies inflicting damage for a "higher cause." The Inquisition, the pogroms, and the jihads are examples. Most wars, fought for principles such as protecting or uniting the homeland, or for national honor, are examples. The father who beats a child "for their own good" is an example. And the mother ignoring such abuse "in order to keep the family together" is an example. In the Bible, Abraham's willingness to kill Isaac because it is "the will of God" is an example.

Our history is replete with evil done in service to principles such as honor, justice, love of country, and even love of God. Souls who do damage in the name of high values and holy words feel immediate confusion in the landing and healing places. They are able to hear and feel love but only mediated by things they already believe. For example, souls who believe in a God of severity and judgment may not be able to see the compassion and support that's all around them. Souls who believe in revenge, punishment, and "eye for an eye" may simply be deaf to the gentle voices of guides soothing and ministering to them. They expect to be shouted at so nothing else can be heard. For a time they may go to a dimension where things are as they expect until the story line, borne of these old beliefs, can be gradually changed.

TIME TRAVELERS

Some souls arrive at the gate having spent little time in the present moment of their lives. They lived in their past, reviewing old sins and mistakes; they lived in the future, imagining either great disasters or great triumphs. These souls—always ahead or behind the present moment—encounter special problems after death. They struggle to see what's actually there and are either slipping back to re-experience moments of the just-completed life or imagining a future in the spirit world that's unlikely to happen. So they pedal back and forth between past and future, ignoring the love that's all around.

Because time travelers aren't good observers of the present, they need a period to experience quiet, nonthreatening images. They may live in gardens—as I first encountered in the landing place—or soothing rooms with windows giving beautiful views. They may be given energy baths that are intensely pleasurable and akin to sexual feelings on Earth. The bath focuses attention on the present, and in that state they are more likely to hear the sound of love.

OLDER SOULS
AND THE DIRECT FLIGHT

Souls who've lived many lives have experienced the passage from a physical body to being in spirit hundreds of times. They more easily recognize that they have died, remember and allow the tug toward spirit, and may cross directly into the arms of guides and loved ones. They know the routine and what to expect. They are attuned to love. The hallucinations suffered by emotionally disturbed or less experienced souls are not their fate.

These more advanced souls have worked through many karmic lessons. Their lives—while often marked by pain and great challenges—were guided by a sense of mission and spiritual truth. They were not lost or alone. They saw through the amnesia and didn't forget that Spirit lives with and in them. As a result, many make the direct flight to a soul group and quickly resume their work—often learning special skills—there are many careers in the spirit world—that they will utilize on Earth or after they've stopped incarnating. These souls may not pause for a full life review but will, in time, consult with guides about the life just lived.

HOW TO SPEND LESS TIME IN THE BARDOS

There are things you can do now to have a more direct flight after death. Layovers on Earth, in the healing place, or in the "strange dimensions" can be minimized by doing these six things:

1. *Prepare now to recognize when you are dead.* While out-of-body and near-death experiences are not rare, most of the time when you're outside of your body, you have crossed over. Pay attention to the events surrounding your out-of-body experience. Are lifesaving efforts continuing? Are people mourning? Are they wrapping or cleaning your body? Also note how long you have been out-of-body. If a lot has happened and significant time has gone by, your incarnation is likely over.

2. *Feel and accept the tug up to Spirit.* If you are out-of-body, pay attention to the tug toward Spirit. It may show up as a desire to "let go," it may come as a movement upward, or it may simply arrive as a graying out of the physical scene of your death while your conscious awareness continues. However it shows up, allow it. Encourage it. Accept and go with it.

3. *Trust that you will be guided and cared for.* From the moment you leave your body, guides are closely attending to you. Expect them. Trust that they are with you, even if you can't see them. Let them take you where you need to go. They love you; they have only your best interests at heart. Their sole job is to care for you.

4. *Listen for a voice or words in your mind.* Your guides will very soon start communicating telepathically. In some cases, the guides communicate with a simple awareness, a sense of knowing. Put your full attention to hearing whatever they convey.

5. *Avoid forming mental images or pictures.* This often leads to disturbing visions that plague souls just arriving in spirit. Instead, *focus on your feelings of love for souls who've already crossed over.* You'll see them soon. Anticipate that and keep your attention on love. Feel it. Listen for it.

6. *As soon as you see guides or loved ones, attend fully to them.* Listen to them. Feel the love flowing between you. Love is your passport. When you feel it, you won't wait long before entering the spirit world.

CHAPTER 4
Life in Our Soul Group

WHEN I GOT TO MY SOUL GROUP—the farm—everyone greeted me, incarnate or not. There was a celebration of return, of finally joining my divided soul energy back together after my life as Jordan. That pause to welcome me was like recess at school. Everyone was playing. Everyone was throwing love at me. But when recess was over and I was safely ensconced back in the group, our work resumed.

Soul group work is learning. We learn in three ways: class work, where we learn from teachers; individual tutorials, where guides give us special training focused on our own past lives and past choices; and field trips, where we acquire special advanced skills to prepare for a spiritual career. More on this in a moment.

PLEASURE FOR SOULS

Learning is only part of the experience in spirit. There's actually more fun in the afterlife than on Earth. In the physical world, pleasure is experienced in the nervous and limbic systems. It peaks and then quickly decays as we desensitize to the experience. Our bodies can't retain sensations of pleasure for very long because our arousal system is designed to return to baseline quickly. In the spirit world, enjoyment can be sustained indefinitely because it doesn't depend on bodily reactions. So on one hand, our joy in spirit doesn't match up with the brief, star-spangled intensity of orgasm (and truthfully many of us miss that). But on the other, we can hold deep, sustained enjoyment through experiences such as:

+ visiting and connecting to soul friends
+ intimate merging
+ tourism—visiting other worlds, other times, and other stages in the development of consciousness
+ meditating on the *love of all* (more on this later)
+ creating—everything from music to energy sculptures to planets

EACH SOUL'S LESSON PLAN

Souls have an individual lesson plan. Even souls in the same group, like the farm, have unique learning objectives. While guides may teach certain lessons collectively, much of the knowledge we acquire is through study of the Akashic Record (the history of every life, every event, every choice made during incarnations—both as it happened and as it *could* have happened).

Studying the Akashic Record—sometimes alone, sometimes with guides—is the primary way we review and learn from each incarnation. We examine with great attention every choice and each word spoken as if it were happening now, studying how it affected ourselves and others, feeling the impact of anger or of love. And then we open chapters in the Record that reveal what could have happened if we made different choices. These "might have been" scenarios allow us to witness an alternative life, viewing it much as we would a movie, except we can peer into the deepest, most hidden reaction of each character in the plot. These alternate realities are animated only as long as we examine them. When we move our attention to something else, they go dark, returning to a mere potential state. It's like the moment when you stop reading and close the pages of a book. The action stops; the story ceases.

We also study the Akashic Record to learn the intricacies of cause and effect, watching years-long sequences of events all flowing from a single choice. A single moment. A father slapping a child and yelling, "You're bad!" can launch a ripple effect that will churn through generations. But we don't just study the effects of human action. We examine every instrument of change: how water erodes rocks in a stream, how freezing and unfreezing rain in the cracks of granite causes mountains to rupture, how the Big Bang pushes matter ever further into entropy, the silence of nothingness. We can look at cause and effect on every level so that eventually souls can recognize the underlying force driving every phenomenon, be it physics or human behavior.

Related to the laws of cause and effect—and also studied in the Akashic Record—are the *laws of change*. These principles guide conscious interventions that allow souls to interrupt cause and effect and rechannel the course of human events. In the same way a dam can alter a river's flow, laws of change, judiciously applied at a moment in time, can redirect history. I spend a good deal of time in the afterlife studying the laws of change because some of my work, in future incarnations, will be to apply this knowledge to give a small push to the flow of Earth events.

The laws of change greatly resemble the martial art of judo. An attacker's strength and momentum, with the slightest shove, are redirected. The hurt that might have happened is sent in a harmless direction. This art can be practiced on many levels: a small, unexpected word of compassion can suddenly defuse a conflict; a single sentence ("Give me liberty or give me death") can galvanize a country, or a simple idea (restorative justice) can save one.

Masters of the laws of change often incarnate specifically to redirect damaging vectors of cause and effect. Souls like Lincoln, Gandhi, Gorbachev, and Christ gave a small push and forever changed the forces that shape human destiny and consciousness. While my work focuses on change (as well as teaching and guiding), other souls are learning to become healing masters, creators (making matter out of energy), life givers (starting with primitive forms of consciousness), librarians (collecting the knowledge and gained experience from each soul into a central databank—collective consciousness), organizers and leaders, and many other roles.

These spiritual careers are nurtured with special one-on-one tutorials with guides and field trips to places where we can do apprentice work. All this training (class work, tutorials, and field work), plus all the recreation we enjoy, is overseen by guides. We have choices, but in much the same way parents structure their children's lives, guides create our schedules and shape our activities. They are the teachers and principals in our schools and our camp counselors when we're having fun. Because the afterlife has no day or night, no natural periods for work and rest, and no need to eat or sleep, the patterns that shape our life on Earth are missing. We need guides to create these structures for us.

WHAT WE DO IN THE AFTERLIFE

Our lives in the spirit world are multifaceted—just as they are on Earth. What we do keeps changing, so we are never bored. To understand what it's like in the afterlife, you have to realize how much souls love learning. That is our purpose, our mission. We were created for this one reason—to absorb knowledge and experience, and give it to *all*. We incarnate into a physical universe to learn from that; we love each other and learn from that love and connection; we develop expertise at our spiritual careers. Everything we do fills us with an ever-increasing sense of truth. We never arrive at truth. No one does, not even the *all* (collective consciousness). We keep moving toward truth—holding more and more of it—but never arriving.

A "day" in the afterlife—every moment of it—is spent loving and learning. And remember, we can do multiple things at once, so much of what we do is simultaneous rather than sequential. For example, I can visit my loved ones who are still incarnate while at the same time deeply studying the Akashic Record. Or I can be listening to a guide give a lecture while being a tourist on another planet and learning from the life forms there.

Activity level in the spirit world varies depending on whether you're currently incarnate. Souls are less active in the afterlife when their energy is split—some remains in a physical body, and some remains behind in their soul group. While less active, incarnate souls remain engaged with their soul group and continue some of their learning activities. You might think of it as taking a smaller course load in college (heaven) when you also take a job (incarnating to a life on Earth).

So with this in mind, let me list some of the activities I'm involved in.

+ Visiting much loved souls. While we can communicate telepathically across infinite distance, it's like talking on the phone. Something is missing. It feels much more complete when souls are next to each other so their energy can mingle and flow back and forth. I spend a lot of time (more on time in the next chapter) visiting soul friends and family. The conversations—like all communication in the spirit world—take place through the medium of love and are deeply pleasurable. There's a lot of sharing, just like we do on Earth, of experiences and things we've learned. For example, when I visit with my dad from my last life (Matthew) here in the afterlife, we spend a lot of time trying to derive principles and master concepts from what we've observed in our lives. We share a fascination with figuring things out.

+ Connecting to embodied souls. Communicating to loved ones who are still incarnate is a challenge. The vibrational levels, as noted before, are so different that direct communication is often impossible. Any time a soul on Earth thinks of me, it opens a channel, and if they are receptive, I can answer telepathically. Literally this involves planting thoughts by subtly stimulating neural pathways in the brain. It's a skill that some of us are better at than others. And some can't do at all.

Sending part of my energy to visit (through the "hall-ways of light," see chapter 11) makes telepathic communication stronger. I can also manipulate electricity to send signals and messages, or I can enter dreams. I stay in very close contact with souls I love on Earth—watching over them, guiding them, reassuring them, and sending love. Caring for and supporting incarnate souls from my spiritual family is a core part of my work as a soul. When they need me, I am there. And I have taught them, more and more, how to listen for me.

+ Connecting to *all*. Part of my time is spent in a kind of meditative state, where I connect to collective consciousness. It's like turning on a radio in which you hear the broadcast for every channel simultaneously. Knowledge fills me, as does this deeply peaceful sense of being part of the whole, of belonging through love. All souls do this. And as souls advance and develop, they connect to *all* more often. Eventually, they may do this for the majority of their time.

+ Reviewing lessons from past lives. Again, this is all done through study of the Akashic Record. Guides are often involved, directing our attention to moments of choice while showing (1) how the choice affected everyone involved, and (2) what would have occurred had a different choice been made. The focus, for any given session, is usually a single theme. For example, how we reacted to anger. Or what we did in the face of loss. Whatever this theme, related choices are often examined across several lifetimes.

+ Creating things. Most souls engage in some creative activities. For me it is music. I invent "sounds" using energy—raising and lowering vibrational frequencies in a unique pattern. I can mimic certain instruments on Earth, or project sound patterns that no physical instrument has ever produced.

  Some souls create images—akin to painting or sculpture on Earth—that capture a form of truth and beauty, which are really the same thing. Others are storytellers; others find creative ways to teach or demonstrate spiritual skills; still others create life forms, and develop new atomic particles, new forms of matter, or even new laws of physics (in preparation for the next, more perfect universe). A lot of souls work on developing new healing processes—something very important since incarnations on Earth can be so painful and disruptive to soul energy.

+ Rituals. Our soul group doesn't eat together like families do on Earth, but we do connect ritually. We take time, periodically, to do a form of singing that synchronizes our energy patterns for a while, and helps us feel closer. We do ritual merging—sometimes as a group to strengthen the emotion of belonging and sometimes in pairs, where we experience a deep intimacy and knowing of each other that feels energetically similar to sex.

+ Lectures and seminars with advanced souls. Part of our training involves being exposed to the wisdom, skills, and experience of advanced souls. We look forward to these lectures because they give us a glimpse of what we are becoming and dimensions of spirit that we don't yet know. I am filled with energy and love when advanced souls teach us. It's like getting to go backstage to meet your favorite band or getting to stand before a great teacher like Sathya Sai Baba or Krishnamurti.

+ Movies. These are special "videos" from the Akashic Record that form amazing travel logs. We can watch the Big Bang, we can see the formation and evolution of previous universes, we can watch documentaries of life forms who host incarnating souls on other planets, and we can peer down the timeline to future events. We also watch and learn from documentaries of souls who have led inspiring lives.

+ Enjoying "the darkness." We don't sleep, but we can enjoy periods alone and draw a sort of cover over ourselves. We can have our own thoughts, our own memories, and our own hopes and plans in privacy—there's no telepathic seepage of our thoughts to other souls.

+ Skills training. As described earlier, there are many spiritual careers. After we've been incarnating for a while, and we're not using all the time between lives to review and learn from our most recent incarnation, guides begin encouraging us to consider a career in the spirit world. I'm learning how to influence incarnates with dream images, channeled thoughts and suggestions, memories, and feelings of love. Guides oversee and coach me to use these skills with embodied souls, ranging from people I know intimately to complete strangers. I've learned to watch for little surges in the human nervous system that show my implanted thoughts are being heard.

+ Sitting. We don't actually sit—unless we conjure a chair energetically. We use this term within my soul group to mean just being together. Our collective energy is like a low murmur, a conversation that doesn't quite reach the level of words. But in that murmur is a deep belonging. Elisa—whom I've partnered with many times on Earth— says it's like when we lay in bed just holding each other. A perfect attunement.

The soul group is our family, our classroom, and our main source of strength and belonging. We learn together, reincarnate together, and nourish each other with love. The activities I've just described are part of daily life. We aren't playing harps, sitting on clouds, or drinking grog in some Viking Valhalla. We aren't living in mansions or walking in sandaled feet on the courtyards of temples. We are just a group of souls who learn and love together.

PREPARING TO MEET YOUR SOUL GROUP

The people you love most, with whom—from the very beginning—you had a sense of comfort and familiarity, are likely in your soul group. You have lived many lives together, and you are connected with a deep, eternal bond. Expect to see them soon after you cross over. In fact, you can ask now for the loved souls you want to greet you. They will be waiting for you. Prepare for that meeting by remembering who they are now. List whoever you think is in your soul group—your intuition is most probably right, but there will be some surprises.

CHAPTER 5

Time

TIME EXISTS BOTH on the physical plane and in the spirit world. The sole function of time is to mark change. Time would stop if nothing moved, if nothing evolved. On Earth, time marks physical changes—the hands of a clock move, the tide wears away rocks, a car speeds from Boston to New York, and lines of age form on the faces of loved ones. In the spirit world, time marks changes in consciousness, the growth of awareness, the before and after of a thought, and the birth of a creation. Time reflects both the personal development of each soul and the evolution of collective consciousness as it, too, continues to grow and create.

God (collective consciousness, *all,* the whole, the Divine) exists in time because God continues to learn and expand. There is no end to consciousness becoming. Consciousness will always become larger, knowing what it didn't know before, creating what before it couldn't create. Full knowledge—complete and absolute—doesn't exist now, nor will it ever. Time stretches infinitely, marking each thing learned as consciousness changes.

While time in the spirit and physical worlds functions to mark change, spirit world time is both outside of, and independent from, physical time. From the spirit world, we can observe our universe at any point in its history, as well as previous, less perfect and evolved universes. We can watch the Big Bang and the implosions of the first stars. Through special volumes of the Akashic Record, we enter those events in the same way we step inside an Imax theater on Earth.

While we can watch the evolution of our universe like a 3-D, 360° movie, we can't literally travel to many of those events because our soul energy can only go where hallways of light have been formed to carry us. There are vast regions and eras in the universe that have no passageways and no means for us to reach them (more on this later). So while we can view anything that's happened in all of history, we can only *visit* where the roads take us.

To physically enter any planet or dimensional plane in the universe requires a body, so we must incarnate to visit. And we can only incarnate into appropriate places, times, and organisms. As far as incarnating on Earth, we can become embodied at any time in human history. A soul can incarnate successively in the 1920s, the Stone Age, a metropolis in the year 2300, or ancient Rome.

Physical time is elliptical rather than linear. If you think of the starting point of our universe as one end of the ellipse, the point farthest from the start (on the far end of the ellipse) is the last moment in the existence of the last galaxy. But if you keep going around the ellipse, you can go back in time and return to the Big Bang. That's what physical time looks like from the spirit world; it's why we can navigate forward and back to enter any point in human existence.

While it's possible to incarnate at any time, souls usually find it too disruptive. We generally prefer to let our own soul development run in parallel to Earth time. Most souls don't like to be thrust into an environment totally different from anything they've known. This tendency is what creates the impression among past life regressionists that the developmental process of the soul, and its incarnational sequence, is bound up in Earth time. But this isn't true. Souls have the option to have their next incarnation at any time in human evolution or in the evolutionary history of other inhabited planets. It's just unusual souls who choose to do so.

THE MATRIX OF CAUSE AND EFFECT

The matrix holding every life, every choice, and the effects of every choice—from the beginning of human history to the end—can be seen in the spirit world. The entire ellipse of Earth time is known. And yet, paradoxically, souls enter a body, a family, a culture, and an era with free will to make choices and learn from everything they do. While the outcome of these choices—in the form of cause and effect—has occurred even before a soul enters a particular body, their choices are still made freely and naively, and what they learn is new, never before known by the individual soul or collective consciousness. So again, while each choice is freely made, the actual choice and its outcomes are already known.

TIME AND YOUR
SOUL'S DEVELOPMENT

Souls who incarnate are likely to do so hundreds of times. Many lives are short and difficult—abbreviated by illness, injury, or violence. But each life is chosen for what it can teach and for experiences that are aligned with the soul's karmic lesson plan. Souls spend thousands of Earth years incarnating and gathering from these lives knowledge that could only be gained in the physical universe.

Between lives, time is measured not in years but by what is learned from the Akashic Record and in tutorials that train us for spiritual careers. As souls evolve and advance in wisdom, their aura changes, and this, too, is a way time marks us. In the same way the lined faces of people are reminders of their years of experience, auras of a darker, richer color bespeak soul wisdom.

ELASTICITY OF TIME

The presence of love and beauty changes the experience of time. On Earth, the experience of falling in love expands time. Days seem to stretch endlessly because they are filled with intimacy and discovery. The contemplation of beauty also expands time, as we subjectively experience it as slowing. We gaze at glacier-cut mountains and time seems to stop.

In the spirit world, love and truth and beauty (essentially the same thing) have a similar effect on time. During periods when we merge with *all*, we experience a suspended oneness as we are flooded with knowledge and belonging. That oneness *is* love, composed of the most profound truth and beauty. As souls are absorbed into oneness, time expands to the point of irrelevance. Time—while we are merged with *all*—disappears.

TIME AND THE INFINITE

Because our souls have a beginning, there was a time before our soul existed, and there is an infinite amount of time that stretches after our soul's "birth." We can learn about the time before our beginning in the same way we learn about history before we were born on Earth. We can study it in books and "movies" (the Akashic Record). But we can also "drop in" to places where the hallways of light allow us to bring our soul energy, and in those places we can navigate back and forth on the ellipse of time. We can't go everywhere, or to every historical moment. We can only go where the pathways exist to transport our energy.

Let's say, for example, that a certain planet became uninhabitable and died, and the hallway of light is gone that once transported souls to that place. You could observe that planet—through a form of the Akashic Record—as it was. You could watch and study its history. But you couldn't bring your soul energy there to have the immediacy of direct experience. It's the same thing as an archaeologist studying drawings and maps of a ruined temple. They can learn a lot but never stand in the temple as it once was.

Because all souls are eternal, our time continues in a forward, linear march forever. But some of the future is hidden from us. We cannot look forward in spirit time (as we do the elliptical time of our planet) to see the next, as yet uncreated universe.

What has not yet been created does not exist in spirit. What has not been learned is not yet known in spirit. What has not yet been thought is a void in the collective consciousness of spirit.

Spirit (God, collective consciousness, *all,* the whole, the Divine) keeps creating new and more perfect universes for one reason: to learn. Like a dad too big to fit into his daughter's playhouse who must ask her what it's like to be inside, Spirit sends souls, small pieces of consciousness, into the universe it created to learn from interacting with its laws and forms.

Consciousness is energy. And thought, a directed form of consciousness, is energy. Consciousness, through directed thought, turns energy into material dimensions with unique laws and forms. Consciousness creates these material dimensions—universes—to play with and learn from. And we—small fragments of collective consciousness—are learning machines that enter the universe to discover everything it has to teach.

Collective consciousness cannot enter and occupy the universe on the micro level in the same way that we can. There is much the universe has to teach that can't be understood from the nonphysical vantage of pure thought.

When everything has been learned from the universe we now occupy, it will be archived—like a beautiful but already read book—and the next one will begin to form from the primordial energy of collective consciousness. Collective consciousness *must* create in order to evolve. In the same way the creation of the wheel was necessary to spawn forms of transportation we'd later invent, the creation of each universe sparks unimaginable growth and learning by spirit.

We are a central and necessary part of the evolution of spirit. As souls mature, they are more frequently merged with *all* (God, Spirit, the whole, collective consciousness). They contribute to the knowledge, the thoughts of *all that is*. There will always be new and beautiful creations and new truth. And as consciousness grows, there will be a deeper resonance of love connecting every thought, every soul. Time will continue, but as a flower—a blooming of consciousness in greater and greater perfection—forever.

You can prepare to merge with *all* right now, on Earth. Two things will come of it. The first is a sense of an awareness of love, which is the foundation of consciousness, as well as a sense of our connectedness and relationship to *all that is*. The second is a preparation for experiences you will have in spirit, where a cyclic merging with *all* is central to a soul's development.

There is a place inside that is neither desire nor seeking nor acting. It is silent and empty. It is waiting. It is the moment before deciding, before acting. It is the loneliest place, but it's also the portal to *all*.

Meditation
for Merging with *All*

Some people access *all that is* by chanting "I am." But the doorway is through awareness of "I"—the infinite life of your soul, including all that it has felt and learned and all that it has seen. At the center of the most alone place in the "infinite I" is the doorway to *all*. The doorway opens to every soul we love and the all that holds and teaches us.

By meditating on your separateness, you feel the walls dissolve. You are touched by a thousand hands. A thousand voices whisper to you. The wisdom gleaned in a thousand lives enters you. It all becomes your strength, your fortitude to come back to the body, to go on living.

The *all* is the light surrounding us. To get there, go deep inside your single point of light, your "me-ness." Recall and feel the trajectory of your individual life. Where has your soul been going? What have you been learning? Allow your memory to drift back, stopping at random places—it doesn't matter where. All the memories you recall will get you where you need to go.

Now, after pausing to enter these random memories, wait. Feel. Allow a sense of yourself to bubble up. Stay with that—the feeling of being a star in a universe in which there are such great spaces between the points of light.

In this feeling, you can find the *all*. The *all* surrounds you, whether you sense it now or not. Imagine your star, your single point of light, surrounded by other stars. When you are ready, your attention will shift to the points of light that surround you. They are made of the same stuff as you. The distance is *nothing*. The *light* is what matters. The light is love, connecting everything.

The *all* feels like relief, surrender, and letting go. The pain and loneliness disappear. It is becoming, for a moment, not just the ocean bather but the ocean itself; not just the driver but the road and the destination; not just the lover but the beloved; not just a star but every star and all the light in the universe. The moment is brief. It is like a chime that sounds once, but the echo goes on and on.

USING TIME IN THE SPIRIT WORLD

When souls choose a body in which to incarnate, they are shown lines of probability—what is likely to happen based on the matrix of cause and effect at the moment of birth. They are given an idea of how long they will live and some of the physical, emotional, and environmental challenges they'll face. But from the moment of birth on, these lines of probability become less and less predictive. Each choice that souls make changes them and alters—sometimes a little and sometimes a lot—the matrix of cause and effect on Earth.

While every choice is free and changes the matrix, *the matrix already contains the effects of those changes and choices.* Yet the soul's choice isn't preordained. Rather, the ellipse of Earth time already holds it; the choice was known and its effects recorded before it was made.

Souls do not study the matrix of cause and effect for a particular life before they enter it. To do so would influence free choice and rob them of lessons that can only be learned by naively facing an unknown future. Guides and discarnate souls don't share the future with embodied souls for the same reason—important lessons would be lost. Time teaches us, as incarnate souls, by hiding the future. And time teaches souls in spirit by forbidding knowledge they haven't learned.

The "fruit" of the tree of knowledge in Genesis isn't knowledge of good and evil—there is no such thing—it is knowledge of the future. When we break the amnesia we're born with and seek knowledge of what will be tomorrow, we are losing our mission here. We are "cheating" in this planetary school that relies on not knowing what will happen.

Forget soothsayers and psychics who promise you a picture of what is to come. They will not help you in your mission. Their prognostications are mostly lies. And if they were the truth, they would take from you what's most precious for your learning—the unknown.

In the spirit world, we use time to learn how consciousness evolves, how it constantly seeks a truth that will fill the voids between what is known. The darkness, what is not yet known, is empty of thought and awareness. Where the emptiness resides is where collective consciousness seeks to fill, asks where there is not yet an answer, creates where nothing has ever formed. Time is the measure of this process; time holds every next thing; time is the length and breadth of God—all God has thought and all God has done. So time—in the spirit world—is the evolution of all discovery.

CHAPTER 6

Love

LOVE IS A PLACE, A LOCATION. It is where consciousness resides. It isn't a feeling, or a state, or a form of experience. It is the place of all thought, all knowledge, all truth. It is the essence of beauty and what moves us to recognize beauty and know love in the presence of beauty.

Love is joining; it is the act of seeing, knowing, and, for a time, becoming the beloved. Love is a place of pure belonging where we *enter* each other and, finally, the whole. Love is not a subject and object nor is it a lover and a recipient of love. It is the place where they live together, having the same awareness, the same memory, the same truth.

Love on Earth has only moments of such merging because we are separated by our skin, our needs and fears, and the alien quality of "otherness" that we can never fully overcome. We are opaque, and cannot fully let in the love and energy of others like we can in the spirit world. On Earth, we have only a visceral knowing of the hope and pain and desire that lives, like the beating heart, inside the other.

Love in the spirit world—that place of merging, knowing, and belonging—lives as a shadow, a faint presence inside of us. That shadow is the source of our loneliness here on Earth.

55

Love on Earth is an endless yearning for the love of spirit that has been largely forgotten.

Our Earth body can hold so little love that we are afraid of it. We numb ourselves to it. We turn it into physical arousal or release. Or we make it holy and untouchable, so pure it becomes a chilled breath rather than a place to live. This isn't our fault; it's simply because of the loneliness we live with. We can only feel the faintest echo, in the briefest moments, of what love in spirit is really like.

THE EVOLUTION OF LOVE

This is why we're here: to discover love. The Divine—the whole, *all that is*—could not love when it was one undifferentiated consciousness because love is an experience that requires duality. It occurs at the junction of two or more consciousnesses.

So the Divine had to divide into parts—souls, oversouls, conscious entities—in order to experience love. But there was a problem. In the spirit world, love has an automaticity. It just happens because the entities, while separate, are also fused into one. The love isn't forged, chosen, or created because the "all are one" experience makes love necessary, determined, and unchosen. While deeply satisfying and very beautiful, even blissful, this uncreated, unchosen love is incomplete.

Only with complete separation (an illusion formed by our incarnation on Earth and other planets) can love finally be created intentionally and fully evolve from stasis (something that just is) to something that generates and grows. Our journey here and the aloneness our souls feel in this place is a necessity for the evolution of love. The Divine grows in its knowledge of love as we do. The trajectory of consciousness on Earth is moving from selfishness (protecting and preserving the life of the individual) to community to oneness. All fueled by *intentional* love.

There are hundreds of ways to manifest love on Earth— healing, holding, community building, protecting, teaching, cleaning, beautifying, giving, joining, sacrificing, witnessing another's pain, caring and supporting in the face of pain, yearning, grieving, taking a blow meant for another, paying attention or seeing, surrendering, compassion, and so many others. Most of these forms of love are unavailable in the spirit world, but they teach lessons we couldn't learn otherwise. All of them advance the conscious discovery of love.

AWAKENING TO THE LOVE YOU HAVE

Love always starts with seeing what is. Your body breathes; it moves; it feels. Love on Earth starts with inhabiting your body, accepting and nourishing it, and fully experiencing all that it gives. Some sensations hurt and some feel good, but they are all doorways to life. Some emotions are painful and some excite us, but they are also doorways to life.

Seeing what is leads to loving what is. In us and around us are things we don't see or accept and so cannot yet love. Similarly, what we push away or resist, we cannot love, and these painful things only become more painful. When we turn toward the painful thing, we see it and start to love it.

Love reveals its beauty and changes the pain into a source of life.

How do you love the pain in your knee? First, you come to know the pain by observing and not running from it. The pain reminds you of the beauty experienced in walking, in moving. It reminds you that the body is finite and fragile. This is what your body is, and you see that it's precious. The body moves more slowly, carefully, and this experience becomes beautiful, a reminder to be grateful.

How do you love the pain of loss? First, you turn toward it. You allow yourself the feeling. You don't bathe in pain, but rather you observe it until you feel the preciousness of what's no longer in your life. You feel your love for it, your gratitude for it. And now you carry that love and gratitude with you along with the sadness. It is in your blood. You feel alive because you love all that is present and all that is gone.

How do you love the person who hurts you? You *see* them—their pain and fear, hope and desire. You see that they are like you, inhabiting a difficult world. They thrash about, trying to survive. They are failing and learning, learning and failing just as you are. You can love them for being here—with you.

LOVE IN THE SPIRIT WORLD

In the spirit world, everything we see we know. And everything we know we also love. That's why, in spirit, we are surrounded with love. Every aspect of the spirit world is a thought derived from the whole (all of us). And every thought from the whole is a small sliver of all the truth and beauty that is.

Love feels safe when we are in spirit. There is nothing we need to hide because there is no judgment or rejection. There is nothing we need to pretend because everything we are is seen and accepted. The pain of being exposed and being perceived as bad or wrong doesn't exist. We just are. As individual souls, we drift among our peers as glass houses— absolutely transparent. But there are no stones to break us. No swords of contempt to slash us. No list of failures or faults with which to assault us.

We are safe from hurt and therefore can be open, unde-fended, allowing other souls to see us at our core. Since we have no need to protect ourselves, we can see and be seen by every other nearby soul. And each time we experience being seen, we feel energy fill us. Love is being seen and known *at the same time we see and know the other.* It is a form of merging that could be just a brief greeting or it can be a pro-longed joining that allows us to experience each other from the inside.

MERGING IN SPIRIT

There are two ways to merge in spirit to experience love. We can merge in pairs or small groups. It's easy and joyous, and it feels very much like hugging on Earth or like a small group singing together. It feels like a relief from separateness. On Earth, our walls dissolve slowly, with fear and reluctance. In spirit, they are always permeable, always ready to open and allow souls in. The second way we merge is with the whole.

It is like walking into a forest and suddenly *being* the forest. It's like lying on a beach and at once becoming the sand, the waves, and the sky. Becoming everything—all consciousness—is the essence of love because consciousness is made of love. Merging with the whole is knowing the truth of things, the beauty of things. And that knowing creates an energy—a vibrational force—that is the deepest form of connection and love. It is a harmonic so satisfying and lovely that our souls vibrate with it. It is a harmonic so perfect that our souls fill with peace as we absorb a small aspect of *all that is.*

So in spirit, love is a sound, and the sound connects everything. When we see and merge with each other, the sound gets louder. When we enter the temple of the whole, the sound is—literally—*all that is.*

Most souls, even those who are advanced and have lived many lives, can only merge with the whole for a little while. The energy, while beautiful, is more than we can hold over a long period. It's as if we become wires carrying a high voltage. At first, the wire is warm, then hot, then—if the voltage continues—we have to let it go. So we can only stay merged with the whole for a little while: long enough to be warmed by beauty and truth but not so long as to get overwhelmed.

On Earth, the paradox we live with is that we crave love—joining with another—but fear it so greatly that we can only bear it for brief moments, so merging is very challenging. The longer we stay in a merged state, the more we struggle with feelings of dissolving and loss of self. The emotion becomes fear, and we respond by hiding or otherwise disconnecting.

PREPARING TO LOVE IN SPIRIT

We say on Earth that love resides in the heart. In a sense that is true because love is often experienced in the center of the body, in the chest. It resides in our physical core. Love is sent outward from the core and is absorbed into the core of another. And this love is often returned—an *exchange* of vibrant energy.

Our skin and skeletal structures prevent us from physically merging except in a limited way during sex. Embodied souls usually experience love by exchanging—giving and receiving. Love in spirit, as you know now, is the experience of merging rather than exchanging. There are meditations that can prepare you to love in this way—as souls entering each other. Merging can be done here in the physical world—not perfectly and not for long periods—but as a brief glimpse of love in spirit and as preparation for how you'll connect on the other side. These meditations can also deepen and strengthen your relationships on Earth. You can record and do the following meditation alone or together with a loved one.

Meditation for Love through Merging

Focus on your breath, bringing your attention to your diaphragm. Observe the in-breath and out-breath at this place. Count each out-breath until you reach ten. . . . When thoughts arise, let them go, and return to watching and counting your breath. . . .

Now bring to mind a person you love, and see their image. Hold the image for a few moments while noticing feelings of affection or any other feelings that may arise. . . .

Now allow yourself to feel what that person loves, what attracts them, what they care about. Don't worry if you have it right or are making it up. Just feel it, feel it as they do. . . . Take this feeling inside you; let it reside in your chest. . . .

Now allow yourself to feel what that person fears, what they resist and try to get away from. Feel it as they do. . . . Now take this feeling inside you; let it, too, reside in your chest. . . .

Now allow yourself to feel what this person hopes for, what they hope to become, or learn, or have in their life. Feel it as they do. . . . Now take this feeling inside you; let it, too, reside in your chest. . . .

Now allow yourself to sense this person's pain, the emotions they carry that are hard to feel. . . . For a moment let yourself feel these emotions as they do. . . . Take these feelings inside, and let them reside in your chest. . . .

Now allow yourself to sense how this person sees and responds to the world, how they feel *in* the world. . . . Feel their experience of the world as they do. . . . Now take this feeling inside you; let it, too, reside in your chest. . . .

Now let go of all this person's qualities and aspects. Feel their essence, their nature, their soul. Just hold their essence with no idea or concept of them. Take this soul inside you, into your chest. . . . With each breath, take them in; with each breath, hold them with care; with each breath, see the truth and beauty of this soul. . . . Just hold them as they are. . . . Now notice if there is a sense of warmth or energy, and allow that if it's there. Allow yourself to feel gratitude for this soul inside you. . . .

When you are ready, take one more breath, and return your attention to the world around you.

CHAPTER 7

What and How We Learn in the Spirit World

IN THE AFTERLIFE we learn by hearing and absorbing ideas, by observing something new, and by doing things we've never done before. As eternal souls, our very purpose is to learn, to grow more wise, and to slowly transform into beings of greater knowledge and higher vibration.

The lessons of the afterlife help lift us past the karmic struggles of our most immediate incarnation. How do we come to understand the choices we made, the hurt we inflicted, the losses we endured, and the blows that staggered us? In the afterlife, we have time to make sense of every moment of the life just lived. We can watch every word we spoke, every gesture, and every intention to see its effect. Did we respond with love, or were we focused on our own desires, our own pain?

Those hours of that life come back to us. We recall each choice as if it were happening in the present and feel the effect of each act of anger or of love. The hours come back to us howling with loss or allowing us to sink into the reverie of love and connection. We live that life not once but many times. We stand to make our vows and then break them many times. We see the choices, the moments of rejection or embrace, the falls or the moments of lifting-up many times.

We keep watching the hours until we know them, until a quiet comes over us and we accept all that was done or not done. And then we can try again.

The lessons of the afterlife are often the same lessons we incarnated to learn—how a soul loves when love is painful, when the path toward love is scattered with hurt and loss. What we learn on Earth depends on facing pain: a path without obstacles teaches nothing; a vantage point that was achieved without a climb yields no new wisdom. In the afterlife, we digest and make sense of our encounters with pain. Pain shapes us as souls; every mission to Earth or other planets is about seeking love in a jungle of threat, fear, and distraction.

SPECIAL LEARNING OPPORTUNITIES IN THE AFTERLIFE

The entire human history can be viewed from the afterlife. We can observe the smallest choices as well as the thoughts and feelings of every participant in every event. This is data for a spiritual science that combines elements of psychology, history, sociology, chemistry, economics, and the study of individual and mass evolution. We are seeking greater and greater understanding of how souls learn—or fail to learn— in a physical environment. And we are developing greater effectiveness in teaching them via our work as guides and the design of challenging situations and environments that create growth opportunities on Earth.

All the planets on which souls incarnate are elaborate schools. As on Earth, we can study the history of the incarnating species in each of these planetary training grounds. The biological differences among incarnating species and the hugely different physical conditions on these planets create a vast array of learning opportunities. As we methodically observe and study all of this data, patterns emerge and we find new dimensions to the laws of change. We learn more about how individual souls evolve and, by extension, how all of consciousness—the whole—can evolve.

Discovering how things change and grow is the most important science, the most important thought, and the most important work we have.

We also learn in the afterlife by traveling. Tourism is just as important in spirit as it is on Earth. It's a way to gain new experiences and perspectives. Souls can use the previously described hallways of light to visit planets, dimensions, and mental worlds made entirely of energy projected by consciousness. In these places, they can simply observe like a tourist visiting Machu Picchu or Victoria Falls, or they can engage in specific learning tasks such as studying a living culture or doing experimental manipulations of a material environment.

As you can see, planetary learning occurs in three ways. We can incarnate and be subject to the physical laws and environmental challenges of a particular world. We can study the Akashic Record of all that happened—every choice of every soul—in the history of a place. And finally, we can go to that world as discarnate observers with a mission to watch or interact with something specific.

LEARNING BY CHANGING HISTORY

When we study the Akashic Record, we can do more than watch history; we can change history to make alternate time-lines and watch the rolling wave of cause and effect wash across subsequent events and all the people involved. Such changes to history can be as small as altering one minor choice to see its effect or undoing a crucial moment in time to isolate its outcomes. Creating an alternative scenario in the Akashic Record is like opening a book: it is vital and "alive" while you're reading it, but when you close the book and its pages no longer have your attention, this alternate reality recedes into mere potentiality.

LEARNING WITH THE WHOLE

The whole is the mind of all consciousness. That mind has not one thought, but many; not one truth, but the truth of all that has been learned since the first thought. The whole is the holder of everything learned by every soul in every life.

The whole isn't located at a certain spot; it is located where you put your attention. On Earth, you can attend to the pain in your foot, to a particular desire, to a voice telling you something, or to a feeling that pushes you to act. Wherever you put your attention, you have awareness. In the afterlife, we have that same capacity to direct attention. We can recognize all that's around us: we can feel the "essence" of nearby souls, and we can listen to the forms that love takes, but we can also choose to attend to the whole. We can open that door and listen to all that has been thought or known.

Entering that doorway to the whole, to *all,* is no more difficult than a simple choice of bringing our attention there. This connection is like plugging into high voltage. You start buzzing with energy until you direct attention to a particular type of thought, a category of truth, or a kind of experience. "I want to experience what love is like on other planets and dimensions . . . I want to know how men in caves understood Spirit . . . I want to know how life looks through a tribal lens." The whole is like an infinite library and an index to every category of knowledge. How you orient your attention as you connect to the whole opens a subject that begins to download and fill your awareness.

Connecting to the whole is like entering a candy store. It has such sweetness, an intense and overpowering taste that comes from all that is known. And you can lie back and take it in, sinking into the light of all thought, all knowledge. It is orgasmic, a spasm of deep pleasure, but rather than expelling, you take it all in and hold each new thought as a joyous recognition of something true.

When you've spent as much time with the whole as you can tolerate, you are flung out of the vortex, as if by centrifugal force, to remember your individual identity and consolidate all that you've learned with what you already knew.

What you learn when you join the whole depends (1) on what you seek, and (2) on the sturdiness and structure of your "self." If you are chaotic and disorganized inside, or if your internal soul structure is hollow and basketlike in that it holds whatever falls into it, your encounters with the whole will be like a starburst: they will be intense experiences but you will lack understanding of them; you will feel love without direction, without knowing the source. If you are a more experienced and evolved soul, one who has learned much over many incarnations, merging with the whole permits a more focused inquiry and a deeper awareness of love. The merging experience is less overwhelming and can be tolerated longer.

The whole is the ultimate classroom, the ultimate school. Every thought you have connects you to some awareness the whole has gathered. And each moment of such truth goes off like a gong, a deep, penetrating sound that fills you with knowledge. After entering the whole, you are more conscious, more complete, and more able to separate assumption from real experience and truth.

PENETRATING THE DARK— WHAT IS NOT YET KNOWN

Like the dark matter and energy in our universe, the dark of what is not yet known surrounds consciousness. The whole continuously expands—with new awareness and knowledge—into the darkness. The light of our collective consciousness becomes ever brighter, and that light of truth, beauty, and love reaches deeper into the unlit region where there is no thought or awareness.

Everything that souls learn on Earth expands the light. Every struggle and every moment of pain is a lesson that further ignites consciousness. The light burns because every one of us wants to learn better how to love. It doesn't matter whether we succeed in any given life; what matters is that we live trying. Even our failures advance the light.

The lessons we learn as souls, every small gift we give to the great light, come from choices and experiences on Earth and in the afterlife. Whether it's learning how to soothe a child or heal a returning soul's damaged energy, whether it is learning to gather and lead people to a common cause or discovering new methods in the science of evolutionary growth and change, whether it is learning to hold back a sudden thrust of anger or using new variations of natural law to alter the rhythms of a planet, we are each giving what we learn to the mind of *all*.

CHAPTER 8

A Day in Paradise

YOUR AVERAGE DAY IN PARADISE is spent learning, creating, or enjoying. Consciousness does all three. We learn about past lives—what worked and what didn't. Some souls learn about their spiritual career. We practice creating by making music, images that move us, new forms of energy and matter, and new ways of healing. We enjoy belonging to each other and the whole. What we learn—whether about the choices we made in each life or about new spiritual skills—is pleasurable. There is a sense of something filling us, making us more complete. There is an excitement as we can see and do what was not previously possible. Think of a moment when you learned how to make something or when you first understood something amazing about the world or the people in it. The exhilaration filled you for a moment because you understood what was previously unknown. That experience is part of an average day in paradise.

Now imagine the best gathering you've ever attended. It may have been a family event; it may have been a gathering where you felt a sudden sense of belonging, of being seen and understood; it may have been a conversation where you felt joined, known, held in some familiar embrace. That experience, too, is part of an average day in paradise.

Now imagine the last time you completely lost yourself in the moment. You were caught neither in thoughts of the past or future. You weren't trying to solve a problem or chart a course. You were freely flowing in the stream of experience, joyously cascading to the next and the next and the next moment. That is a day in paradise.

Now imagine you're holding your beloved. You are so close that you know that soul's feelings and yearnings. You know what hurts and what soothes that soul. And at once you feel known in the same way. That is every relationship in the afterlife. That is how the embrace of one soul with another feels.

Last, imagine a room that is vast and without any apparent borders. In that room is every soul who's ever existed and every thought, every awareness, everything ever learned or felt. And all of this is connected by the most ecstatic sense of love and belonging. You cannot stay long in that room because the vibration is so high, so intense. But while you are there, knowledge flows into you in a never-ending stream of discovery. You forget yourself, and you are one with all that has been thought and felt. You are the exact opposite of alone; you are at the center of a galaxy in the midst of *all that is*. Any day in paradise can have that. You can be in that room as much or as little as you are ready to be.

The afterlife is not like a city where you choose which streets to go down and which doors to enter. The afterlife is like having the city inside you and choosing which street and which doors of your own consciousness to enter. Every doorway holds something to learn, something to feel, something to create. Each doorway is the merging point between you and each other's soul, between you and the whole.

There is a lamp that is forever lit in the spirit world. It is the lamp of pure consciousness. It is the source of all light, all thought, all belonging, all love. The radiance of that lamp is everywhere—both in the afterlife and even the physical universe. We can see it in the eyes of everyone who is awake; we can see it in the radiant colors of the nebulae. We see it as the gray mists between worlds begin to part and we catch the first glimpse of brilliance on the other side. That lamp light bathes us every day in paradise.

After death, you should expect to see it. And you will.

THE STRUCTURE OF THE AFTERLIFE

The afterlife is both fluid and structured. It is fluid because we are often able to decide what to experience next. This is just like on Earth when you decide whether to do some planting in your backyard or visit your friend, take a walk or have lunch. We make these choices all the time. In the afterlife, we can choose among activities—but with a twist. We can often do several things at once. For example, we can watch over loved ones still on Earth while also studying historical events in the Akashic Record. Or we can travel to other worlds (a kind of tourism) while remaining telepathically connected to a soul friend.

Guides also provide structure by organizing study groups, skill-building and creative exercises, experientials to encounter new thoughts and awareness, recreation, and the like. One way to think about it is to remember your time in college. Some days you spent in classes—very structured explorations of different subjects but with a focus on your major. After class, and on days without classes, your time was more fluid. You visited friends, listened to music, studied, ate, found various ways to entertain yourself, and a lot more. The after-life is like college—but more exciting. You can rest, but you don't sleep. Your consciousness is filled with new thoughts, and the party—your sense of love and deep connection—never ends.

CREATIVITY IN THE AFTERLIFE

We learn in order to create. As each soul gathers knowledge and wisdom over many lifetimes, that knowledge begins to take new shapes and expressions. What starts as pure thought evolves into new, unheard of images, new music, new forms of expression, new ways to heal, new science, new forms of a relationship, and new understandings of consciousness itself.

What is true of individual souls is also true of the whole—all of consciousness. Whatever is learned springs beyond thought, beyond mere awareness, into form. The whole *must* create because thought *requires* form to manifest itself. Such new forms may incorporate energy and light, vibrational patterns (think string theory), images, life forms, the infinite varieties of matter across dimensions, and increasingly more complex and beautiful universes with which to play and experiment.

So an average day in paradise, because we are awake and learning, will always involve some creative form. The most common one is creating images out of energy: a house, a temple, a landscape, a garden, a complex geometric shape, a sculpture. Remember the description of the Victorian house that my soul group lives in? This is one way our group enjoys spiritual architecture, including countless details on the "inside" of the house. The group also creates music and new energy patterns designed to precipitate social change on Earth. All souls and soul groups create like this.

Remember, thought eventually coalesces into form. Every new thought *creates*. Creative expression is an inescapable end product of consciousness, and it is why consciousness *must* continue to grow and evolve.

CHAPTER 9

Envisioning the Afterlife

IN THE PHYSICAL WORLD, we invent images of the after-life that depend on our religious moorings. We have pictures of a God, whether it's the trinity, the God of Abraham and Muhammad, or a multitude of deities and goddesses. None of these pictures resembles the Divine, and souls are often con-fused as they enter the spirit world because they expect to be met by Jesus or Buddha or the Holy Mother. They may be dis-appointed, sensing the absence of these figures. Or they hallu-cinate them, creating images of God and an afterlife that gets superimposed over the real experience.

In some cases, the expectation is so strong that guides cre-ate a Christ or Yahweh or Buddha figure to calm and support an arriving soul. And sometimes, if a soul expects punishment, or conversely, some special reward, these images are presented until the soul begins to see the afterlife as it is.

Souls whose religion leads them to expect judgment are a special problem. Some arrive in the afterlife anticipating a tribunal, and they remain anxious and discontent if no such experience materializes. Where is the thunderous voice of God, they wonder, declaring them fit or unfit for heaven? Where are the angels at the gate who will accept them into God's embrace or cast them into darkness? Nothing like this exists. Souls who are committed to such images may create them for a time, or guides will offer slowly fading judgment scenes until the illusion of judgment is replaced by acceptance and love.

Some guilt-laden souls arrive in the afterlife and create images of fire and burning flesh. Some see demons. Some lie in a state of grief, imagining themselves cast into barren outlands. Others wait, anxious and seemingly alone, for a familiar god or saint to usher them to some sacred place. It may take time, and often an adjustment period in a carefully prepared bardo, for such pictures and expectations to fade.

ENVISIONING THE AFTERLIFE *BEFORE* DEATH

First, let go of all your pictures of God. God is us; God is everything. God's face is our face. God's body is our body. God's thoughts are our thoughts. Because God is all experience, all consciousness, there is no way to put a countenance on that. There is no way to hold a picture of *all that is.*

Next, let go of damnation and hell. There is no such place as hell in the afterlife. As you've learned, souls may remain for a time in bardos where they gradually let go of emotions and beliefs that don't belong in the spirit world. They may, after a life where they've inflicted great pain, choose not to face life review, and they remain cloistered and alone until they do so. But there is no blame or rejection in the afterlife. It is all love, no matter what we did on Earth.

One of the greatest mistakes mystics have made is the suggestion that there is a hierarchy of consciousness—

from consciousness contained only in the body, to etheric consciousness, and finally to multiple levels of spirit or soul consciousness. There is only one consciousness that animates everything. While there are individual soul identities that form a part of the whole, there is no hierarchy where we climb, level after level, to higher and more valued forms of consciousness. So while we remain distinct souls, we are—at the same time—always one.

Souls who identify with or believe they've attained a particular level of consciousness are confused as they enter the afterlife. Where is the stratification? Where is their earned level of attainment? They are looking to take their place on the ladder of spiritual nobility, and there is no such thing.

Rather than distinct castes of soul consciousness, we are all on a continuum of growth and development. Some of us have learned more than others; some souls have developed skills and capabilities different from others. As on Earth, these differences separate souls into groups with similar interests and experiences as well as into groups that have similar spiritual tasks. Some souls spend most of their time in school, learning, just as some young people do on Earth. And most of their relationships are with other "student" souls at a similar developmental level. Some souls are apprentices for spiritual careers, such as teachers, guides, healers, creators, change agents, and others. Some have advanced skills and knowledge and are masters in the practice of their arts. These souls rarely incarnate, and their soul friends are often those who share the same career.

As you see, souls grow and gain knowledge in the afterlife in much the same way that we do in the physical realm. There is a period for learning and preparing, then we use the skills and the knowledge we've gained to do something specific. None of this, however, reflects a hierarchy with fixed levels of consciousness. No soul is more valued than another. We are all just learning and evolving at our own pace.

Whatever pictures you have of the afterlife are so pale and inadequate that they are often harmful rather than helpful upon your arrival. Let your picture of heaven be your image for love: a face that conveys sweetness, a landscape of the heart that holds all within a web of care and support. Let the *feeling* of belonging—whatever image that evokes—be your picture of the afterlife. The feeling of love and belonging leads to the truth of what will come—not clouds and harps, not the soft pastels of artists painting an idealized heaven.

Feel love, the connection of each to all. *That* is the afterlife. The priests and mediums on Earth offer words, which is all they have to give. The truth is in your heart; it is at the core of what you feel for your dearest, your most beloved. *That* is the afterlife.

Often in the moment before death comes the peace. And the peace is the truth of what holds us together. The peace is the breath of love entering us, healing us after a difficult life. It is the essence of what awaits us; the most important thing about the afterlife.

SEEING THE SPIRIT WORLD
AFTER DEATH

As you begin to let go of the physical and feel yourself pulling away, you enter the gray, ephemeral space between worlds.

It is usually experienced as ambiguous, without shapes and edges. And in this realm you can make things up. You can create a whole pantheon of angels and saints, an entire religion. You can create a story where you entered the world for a reason and now leave it full of failure and sin or perhaps pride and righteousness. In the pale light between worlds, you can even find evidence for nihilism, for nonbelief. All things are possible because this place is a blank screen on which you can project anything.

During this migration, the work of the soul is to wait, as a patient seafarer, for the first traces of light. The light is love. Many also hear a sound that is love. Images for your transition are usually handpicked to be relevant to what you enjoyed on Earth and may include cultural or religious icons. Experience it as you would a movie, accepting the scene that's given to you. And, as with a movie, remain passive; let the director (guide) offer the images, introduce characters (loved ones from this past life), and create action. If you start adding things—images of what you expect the afterlife to be, figures of judgment or punishment— you will be confused. Your thoughts and images will collide with the soothing pictures that have been selected for you.

Your work is to let go of all religion, any sense of what should happen, and every hope and expectation. And if fear shows up, try not to attach a thought or picture to it. Just allow the feeling, and let the movie play. To help you prepare, try recording and then listening to the following meditation.

Acceptance Meditation

Focus on your breath, bringing attention to your diaphragm. Observe the in-breath and the out-breath at this place. Count each out-breath until you reach ten. . . . When thoughts arise, let them go, and return to watching and counting your breath. . . . (Pause the recording until you've reached ten out-breaths, then turn it on again.)

Close your eyes now, and imagine looking up into a blue sky. . . . Settle in and watch the sky, and become aware of how the sky and weather always change. . . . You know the weather will be different in a while, and if you wait, some clouds will form . . . and perhaps now they begin to drop a little rain on you . . . and if you wait a little longer, the sun breaks through where the clouds begin to shred . . . and the clouds become orange and gilt-edged in a fading light. . . .

And now the sky begins to get dark. . . . It is ink black except for stars. . . . You stare at the stars . . . and now, way off in one direction, you can see the beginnings of a gray and pink light. . . . Soon it will change to blue . . . a blue sky that in a while will change again. . . .

Now allow the sky to change in any way it will. Don't try to make it do anything . . . just let the sky have whatever weather shows up. . . . Just watch the sky have its weather with complete acceptance. . . . Let it happen . . . (long pause). The sky is life, bringing whatever weather it brings. . . . The sky is the afterlife, and it will not hurt you. . . . It will bring whatever weather it brings. . . . You are just watching, accepting, letting it bring whatever it brings. . . .

When you are ready, take one more breath, and return your attention to the world around you.

CHAPTER 10

Fear of Death and the Afterlife

WE'VE FORGOTTEN WHERE OUR HOME IS; we've forgotten what it's like there. So the thought of leaving this Earth for a place we no longer remember frightens us. The fear of death lives like a cold breath inside so many people, and we run from it in every way we can—through distraction, anger, or drugs, by avoiding even of the thought of death, through rigid spiritual or religious beliefs, through extreme pleasure-seeking, or by building achievements we hope will last—but it's all a vain try at immortality.

The more we seek to avoid death, the more it haunts us, the more it seeps into our hopes and sense of the future. We think death is our biggest problem, but it isn't. Living here with all this pain and loss is the problem, while death is merely a portal to the love and light we have forgotten. We fear death in part because we haven't paid attention to the voices of support and love from the other side. Every day we are encouraged and guided by those voices. But so often we are deaf, focused on our desperate attempts to survive and avoid pain on Earth.

Think of what you've learned in this book from *my* voice on the other side. Death is just a doorway back to our soul group, back to the wisdom we've gained from all our lives, and back to the whole of consciousness that fills us with love and knowledge and connection.

Death often comes with distress and a fog of uncertainty about what awaits us. But that is brief, nothing other than the squeaking hinges of an opening door. Guides and often loved ones show up to help us let go of the material world, to ease us outside of our bones and breath. And even when we are sometimes confused by the transition and hallucinate frightening images or expect punishment, we are led gently toward the light. Even in the bardos, where we gradually let go of old emotions and beliefs, we are watched over, protected. Always, from the moment that death approaches, we are held by souls who love us, and we are ushered—sometimes quickly, sometimes slowly—to our spiritual home.

All this is true. But fear persists because our bodies are composed of matter. And when our material body ceases to sustain life, we fear our consciousness will stop. Our bodies are horrified with the prospect of their own destruction, and this terror infects the soul.

HOW THE FEAR OF DEATH
CAN IMPACT YOUR TRANSITION

Any strong negative emotion must be worked through and softened before full admission to the afterlife. A strong fear of death reduces the vibrational level of our spirit and makes it hard to communicate with souls vibrating at a higher, less emotionally heavy level. For a while, until the fear begins to dissipate, we may feel isolated because we literally can't hear the telepathic messages that surround us.

The feeling of fear typically makes us want to figure out what the danger is so we can make a plan to protect ourselves. This reflex may prompt souls, immediately after death, to begin a vigilant watch for something that's threatening. In the absence of anything material or "real," we start inventing things. Each thought about possible dangers (demons, hell flames, figures of judgment, attacking devils, vast emptiness, utter isolation, bottomless cliffs, rejecting angels, and more) conjures that image. Because we are in a dreamlike state, these visions can take on a very real and threatening aspect. Our guides and loved ones may be "shouting," trying to help us hear or see their love. But fear of death closes our spiritual ears.

What makes fear most problematic, on Earth or in the afterlife, is the role fear plays in separating souls from each other. On Earth, fear divides. It's us against them, us against the dangerous other. In spirit, fear can separate us from the whole, from *all,* and make us feel alone. Love always joins, and fear—love's true opposite—isolates; it denies our oneness.

The fear of death can make the landing place seem dark and empty. Alone and without reference points, fear can become panic. People who panic on Earth often feel as if they are dying (physically and psychologically) and have somehow passed beyond help. They seem alone in their terror. In the spirit world, panic can have a temporary but similar effect.

The disorientation that sometimes follows death, added to an existing fear of this transition, can be especially hard. Do not fight the fear or look for danger. Accept fear as a normal part of suddenly leaving the familiar and the physical. Ride the fear as you would a wave on the ocean.

What to Do When Fear
Grips You Just after Death

+ Trust that soon the wave of fear will pass.
+ Recognize that souls are there to help you.
+ Know that everything will be done to heal whatever pain or emotional wounds you carry into the transition.
+ Be assured that the afterworld is benign and loves you.
+ Be passive. Don't try to figure out or jump to conclusions about what's going on.
+ As described before, wait for the movie to start. Let the guides provide images to comfort and instruct you. They will reach you telepathically with sounds or pictures that convey safety and love.
+ In order to focus away from images of danger, think of all the souls you love, particularly ones in spirit. Call their faces to mind and the feelings you have for them.
+ Simply wait. You will be joined momentarily.

DISBELIEF AND THE FEAR OF DEATH

Doubt and disbelief can inflame fear after death. If you doubt or are unsure if there's an afterlife, but have slipped outside of your body, start by carefully observing your situation.

1. You are still conscious. Your body may have died, but your consciousness has survived. You don't need your body to live.
2. There are certain to be other people like you—now discarnate—and you are likely to meet them soon.
3. You are not in pain; you are able to think and feel and

react. You don't have a body, but the most important parts of you are intact.

4. You may feel fearful, but nothing bad has happened to you.

5. Don't imagine or speculate about things that might happen.

6. Since other souls have survived this transition, and are capable of love on Earth, there will at least be as much love (or more) in the afterlife.

7. Look and listen for love and connection to others right now.

SOFTENING THE FEAR
OF DEATH BEFORE YOU DIE

Your body has served you. It is the lifeboat that carried you across the deep, tempestuous seas of this world. But that body—your lifeboat—is not you. As you awaken to that truth, the fear starts to dissolve. Death loses its aura of danger.

The body cannot love; only the soul can love. The body's attention is fixed on survival. The body becomes *attached* to things that help it survive, but this isn't love. The fact that you love is proof that you are more than the physical; it is evidence that you come from spirit and are part of the whole.

It is through love that the fear of death can soften and fade. Love in every form awakens you to a connection to the whole. And it is love that prepares you for a smoother transit to the afterlife. Very simply, love overcomes fear because it is the bridge to *all,* to spirit, to home. The following meditation will help you prepare by connecting to love.

Meditation to Soften the Fear of Death

The best way to prepare for death is to focus on everything you love—the souls you love, the color of sunset, the sound of wind keening through granite, the moon's path over a lake, the way a cat moves, or how your heart leaps at children's laughter. *Now distill all the objects of your love to the feeling of love, itself.*

- Breathe in the *feeling* of love.
- Breathe *out* the fear.
- When thoughts arise, notice them, and return to your breath.
- Continue breathing in the *feeling* of love and breathing out fear until you have a small sense of calm, of belonging to *all*.
- Whenever the fear of death shows up, use this simple meditation.

Connecting to love in this fashion is the best way you can prepare for the transition to the afterlife. The afterlife *is* love. The meditation leads you to sense the unity of all and to know you aren't alone. Ever.

CHAPTER 11

Navigating

SOULS DO NOT OCCUPY THE SAME LOCATION; they exist, for the most part, with a degree of separation from each other (except when merging). There are a vast number of individual souls, and therefore the spirit world occupies a vast "space." Taken together, the souls and all of the collective energy in spirit comprises the whole, *all,* or God.

MOVING ACROSS THE SPIRIT WORLD

You can navigate the enormous distances of the spirit world by an act of will. But there are no conventional directions, such as up and down, forward and back, because our consciousness shines and sees omnidirectionally. There is no north, south, east, or west as there is on a spinning planet. Instead, we navigate by moving toward unique energy forms. Each soul has an energy signature, and each soul group has a collective energy form. Soul "neighborhoods" are marked by an energy signature composed of the unique soul identities residing there blended with energy created by their collective knowledge.

In addition to the energy markers for individual and collective souls, the spirit world has "locations" for certain categories of thought and awareness. These thoughts exist as part of the whole, as opposed to residing in the consciousness of a particular soul. The physical universe is an outcome and example of creative thought. As a manifestation of consciousness, it resides inside and is part of the spirit world.

When we navigate in spirit, we move toward the specific energy signatures of a soul, a group, a neighborhood, or a manifestation of conscious thought. If we know the unique energy signature, we can always move toward it through the hallways of light. If we don't know it, there are references (the spiritual version of a phone book or data bank) to help us move in the right direction. Knowing what energy signatures we seek helps us move, unfailingly, toward the soul or souls, or manifestation of conscious thought we want to reach.

The hallways of light are energy arteries, and like the veins and capillaries of the human body, they are designed to reach and connect the smallest cell (soul) to the whole. The hallways of light, as previously described, also reach into the physical universe. But in the physical world they are more limited and only go to the places and times we are allowed to visit.

PROPULSION

In the hallways of light, you experience movement with no sense of velocity. You pass clusters of brightness, you pass intersecting corridors, and you pass souls going elsewhere. While you don't consciously navigate, your attention is on the unique energy pattern you seek as a destination. You move toward it as you would move toward a distant mountain on Earth, with your attention fixed, watching it grow larger, correcting course or turning to keep it in view.

Remember, while consciousness (thought) can travel instantly over any distance, your soul energy (the full presence of all that you are, your awareness, your *self*) travels as all energy travels, through space and across time.

The method of propulsion is intention. Intention is a special form of thought that has directional energy. On Earth, intention powers our arms and legs, allowing us to do things, to *move*. Intention externalizes our will, allowing it to take the form of behavior and action. In spirit, intentional energy moves us from one place to another and pushes us across vast spaces in the hallways of light.

The power of intention is inexhaustible. There is no "running out of gas" when it comes to intentional energy. If we want to go somewhere, we can, as long as there are corridors to get us there. The only limit on intention is having sufficient knowledge of the energy signature we seek.

When discarnate souls visit with those on Earth, the most common way is through mere thought. They don't actually travel; their energy remains in the spirit world. But thoughts can easily move back and forth between incarnates and discarnates like a wireless phone. The only necessary conditions are attunement, or actually listening, and the intention to convey a thought. Far less frequent are visits in which discarnates bring their actual soul energy to Earth. These visits usually occur with physical manifestations: perhaps there are sounds, a voice, a visage, or an ethereal body. Such manifestations can't happen without soul energy; a discarnate has to "travel" to the physical plane and skillfully use their energy to get our attention.

WHERE SOULS CANNOT GO:
THE UNKNOWN

Beyond the spirit world and the universes it has created lies the dark unknown. The dark unknown is both something and nothing at the same time. It is whatever collective consciousness—the whole, *all*—thinks that it is, and then it transforms to something else as it gradually becomes lighted and seen. But there is a paradox here: if the unknown can be anything, then it is nothing. The great unknown is like a dream landscape that you can project and make into anything, yet it may become something else wholly unexpected as you take a closer look.

So the spirit world is a vast array of consciousness, of light, bordered by something and nothing—all that is not yet held in conscious thought. As thought expands, as consciousness and the spirit world grow, the dark unknown recedes. As far as we can tell, there are no limits to the dark unknown, because we expect consciousness will continue to evolve and expand into it forever.

The dark, where there is no consciousness, exists in the physical universe as well as in the space that surrounds spirit. We cannot travel into these regions, so even inside a physical universe that was created by the whole, by *all*, there are areas devoid of consciousness that are essentially unknown. It's like having a house and garden but having no knowledge of the space between the walls, above the rafters, or just beneath the surface of the lawn. These are places you don't have access to, and you don't know what's there.

WHAT YOU NEED TO KNOW NOW ABOUT NAVIGATING IN THE LANDING PLACE

Moving in the spirit world requires the harnessing of intention. You don't move *away* from things; you only move *toward* something. So if you don't know where you're going, you don't move.

In the landing place, objects and landscapes are created for you out of energy. You can move toward what you see. But once outside of a constructed scene, movement depends on having a clear sense of destination. You have to know where you're going (or have another soul lead you there). This is how souls can get stuck in bardos—places that have the appearance of a physical world and are used for healing or teaching. Souls remain there because they can't yet conceive of any other destination in the spirit world. They can only move toward the created forms they see, and for a while remain in the bardo because they cannot imagine anywhere else to go.

You can prepare now for navigating in spirit by remembering the unique emotional qualities of the souls you love. These are the Earth equivalents of the energy signatures we move toward in the afterlife. Remembering your love for these souls when you reach the landing place will draw you together. Something important to know is that souls can arrive to help with your transition regardless of whether they are living or discarnate at the time of your death. Living souls always keep some of their energy in the spirit world, which allows them to join you in the landing place.

While you cannot usually remember while incarnate who your guides are, one or more will be present at your transition to spirit. Think of the best teachers and mentors you've known in your life and your feelings of love and gratitude for their guidance. Remembering that feeling will help you see and move toward guides.

In the landing place, always direct your attention toward soul energy—guides and loved ones. The "objects" around you are not important. They are there for comfort or, in some cases, are dreamlike images created by your own mind. These objects and images don't require your attention, and there is no need to move toward them. Instead, move toward the loci of love, the presence of souls (whether you yet recognize them or not) who are emanating joy at your return.

Once you see a guide, you can leave navigation to them for a while. Guides will move you to the next stops in the afterlife until you are fully oriented and ready to make your own way home to a celebration of your waiting soul group.

CHAPTER 12

The Urge to Incarnate

THE SPIRIT WORLD IS A PLACE OF PEACE. There is no pain, as we know it on Earth, coursing through the afterlife. But for many souls there is a hunger for the challenges and beauty of the physical world. We have great fondness for the planets where we've lived. On Earth, I loved the isolated granite peaks and the river valleys chalked with sedge and high grass. I loved holding my partner in a storm of desire. I loved the taste and smell of foods we prepared. I loved learning how to be close, how to share secrets, and how to find solutions to problems. I loved dawn light and the cold wind coming off the Sierras. I loved traveling over great distances and feeling alone among the cliffs and vast spaces of an ocean shore. It was all beautiful to me, and in the spirit world I miss uncovering new things, each a new collision between fear and discovery, between uncertainty and the embrace of life.

Souls remember the beauty of loss, the light of the imperfect, and all that was learned colliding against the hard edges of life. So the planet where we incarnate is like an oft-visited foreign country that we remember with love and yearn to see once more. Though many of our lives may have been difficult, though the physical plane induces much suffering, though our incarnations often involve deep feelings of loss and loneliness, we are still drawn back to visit again.

The lure of physical life includes:

+ Physical sensations not available in spirit: souls remember the warmth of the sun and the joy of exertion.
+ Experiences that please the senses: the unique quality of music, the glory of sunsets, the movement of waves and wind, and the beauty of living things (trees, lichen, our own bodies).
+ Sexual desire and release, hunger and satiety.
+ Touching and holding.
+ Curiosity and discovery.
+ Physical science.
+ Caretaking (of children, of those in need) and service.
+ Risk and adventure.
+ Physical rhythms (tides, day and night, sleep and wakefulness, our breath, our heartbeat).
+ Solving problems, inventing.
+ Creating in a physical medium.
+ Words, including the way they limit what we can say and think while we also strive to expand our expressions and make them more truthful.
+ Weather and seasons.

So despite episodes of emotional and physical pain, there is much that draws us back, much we remember and wish to experience again. The attractions of physical life are not, however, the main impetus for returning. The primary reason for incarnating is to learn, to acquire knowledge and wisdom that can only be found in a physical environment. And the most important of these lessons, as previously described, is to learn how to love without telepathy and merger, without the light, and without direct support from our group and our guides. We must learn how to love while feeling shame and fear, sadness and loss; to love when we are hurt or sick or tired; to love when we are abandoned or rejected; and when we are overwhelmed by the struggle to survive, by threats, or by the imminence of death.

This work can only be done on physical planets, where love must push through each obstacle, each kind of friction and resistance. We are discovering as many ways to love in the face of pain as there are souls learning to do it. And everything we learn adds to the knowledge and wisdom held by *all*.

The essential truth driving us to incarnate is that souls hunger for growth. There are things we cannot discover in the afterlife. We feel a desire to face whatever pain and struggle is necessary to learn those lessons.

THE MOMENT OF CHOICE—YOUR NEXT INCARNATION

We select families, cultures, historical eras, and physical bodies designed to push us toward our own evolution. The process of choosing a next life is done with the help of guides who open the Akashic Record to offer us a glimpse of several possible existences. They show us some of the likely key events of each life and expose some of the innate challenges of living in that body, that family, and that place and time. If, for example, a body will have disabilities or is prey to illness, we will likely be shown that. If major losses occur early in that life, we will likely be shown those as well.

Members of our soul group, or related groups, are given opportunities to incarnate with us into the same family or community. That way, many of our dearest soul friends enter lives in the same time and place so we may continue to learn together. We may incarnate as a group, taking roles in each other's lives—sometimes as siblings, sometimes lovers, sometimes mentors or students, sometimes abusers or antagonists— so that we can reflect back together on all that we've learned. It's a beautiful process when we land in close enough proximity that we will connect in various ways throughout our lives. Then, when we are in spirit, we get to reflect back on each lesson learned in those embodied relationships.

Souls don't take the prospect of incarnating lightly. After difficult lives, they may be reluctant to go back any time soon. Or they may need time to process complex lessons. Souls often take long periods in spirit to strengthen and nourish their soul energy before embarking on the next incarnation. You might think of souls in the afterlife as athletes in training. They have to take excellent care of themselves—getting strengthened with knowledge and nourished by love—before facing their next challenge.

So we wait between lives. We ready ourselves. We digest every aspect of the last incarnation. If we come back too soon, without the necessary recovery period, our soul energy may get overwhelmed by an arduous life or a challenging body. We may arrive on Earth with insufficient resources to deal with its rigors.

Therefore do not, on entering the afterlife, seek a quick

return to Earth. Feelings of failure from a life just completed can tempt souls to reincarnate almost immediately. This is usually a mistake. Settle back into the support and companionship of your group; carefully review the just-completed life with guides; digest what you've learned; and feel the infusions of love that allow and strengthen your soul energy to become more vibrant.

The yearning to incarnate is a necessary and significant part of our soul experience. There's no denying it. But when we have completed our incarnation cycles, we will know. We will feel a letting go of the Earth and the allure of physical life. Until that time, our soul seeks a physical incarnation in the same way we yearn for a loved one. We are drawn toward a feeling of completion, toward a resolution of lessons not yet learned, toward relationships that—over the course of many lives—have yet to be fully realized.

Can you feel your hunger for learning? *That* is the drive to incarnate. Can you feel a sense of something unfinished? *That* is your desire to re-enter life, to sink into the truth of each human relationship until it reveals who you have been and who you are seeking to be.

We stop incarnating only because we have stopped wanting to find knowledge in the physical world. Relinquishing embodiment takes many lives, many roles enacted from the first to the last lines, many thousands of choices that shaped our own and our loved ones' destinies before we let go. When that time comes, we retain only memories of our planet while our attention shifts to the work we've chosen in spirit. And we merge for longer periods with the whole, helping consciousness push further into the dark unknown.

HOW TO CHOOSE A LIFE

When choosing a life, be cautious. Don't act on an impulse. The several lives you will get to review are all going to help you grow. They will be ranked from less to more arduous. This means some lives will have less growth potential along with less pain and fewer challenges. You will also be shown lives that offer great opportunities for growth, but along with that comes significant emotional and physical struggles.

Many souls, out of hubris and overconfidence, choose difficult lives with great opportunities for learning. But the challenges prove too great. The offered lives lead to more significant levels of pain and human desire than the soul's will, resources, and life experience equip them to deal with. The body they are given is too compromised or its cravings too strong. Or it may be that the family, the culture, or the moment in history creates conflicts and demands the soul isn't ready to face.

Be cautious, therefore, of the desire every soul has for growth. Accept a body and a life that won't far exceed your experience and the ability to use your soul energy (will) to steer important life decisions. Historically, some of the greatest human failures, souls who incarnated with good intentions but perpetrated great evil, were the result of over-ambitious choices.

Our growth as souls requires incarnations that are neither easy (safe, comfortable, unchallenging) nor involve skydiving without a parachute. Choose a life that will ask much of you but not more than your soul has the resources to face.

CHAPTER 13

Losses and Reunions

THE DEEPEST TRUTH of the universe is that love is eternal; our relationships to each other and the *whole* go on forever. Reuniting is a myth born of our physical lives. We are always together (even though on Earth we forget), always united in love, always and irrevocably connected to all of consciousness.

So reunion is merely a ceremony where incarnated soul energy returns to spirit, and our soul group and friends bang the drum to welcome us home. But in truth we never left them. Our collective love has always held us as if we were one breath.

We feel so alone on this planet, and the love of incarnates is so tenuous and conditional that isolation seems normal. The emptiness of having our deepest selves unseen (hidden within a body and a personality) is the root of human sadness, and it is why the hope for union animates all our relationships—with both the living and the dead. We cannot know in this place that our aloneness is an illusion created for our own growth.

As we approach death, the thought of reunion often seems more sweet. We have lost loved ones, and even in our most intimate relationships we may continue to feel a distance—as if we have always lived a little apart—beyond being held, beyond being known. And because merging in love is so difficult here, we yearn all the more for it as life reaches its end. Instinctively, if we listen to our soul's truth, we can feel the imminent approach of our joining to all that we love. We can use this hunger for reunion to begin welcoming the transition.

Souls we love who are now in spirit often appear to us in the days or hours before death, when possible, as part of the plan to ease our transition; they remind us that we are going home and there is nothing to fear. This is not the product of a dying brain, anoxia, or the shutting down of body systems. Instead of being a sign of confusion, these visits reflect the clarity that comes as our soul begins throwing off the limiting shell of the body.

So while reunion isn't what it seems (we have always been together), the illusion of being apart, when we are finally released from it, brings a soaring joy. Even in the confines of these bodies and a physical life, we can imagine the return of someone we love and thought forever lost. You've seen the rapture on the faces of families reunited after many years in news stories. That feeling fills our soul as we first glimpse loved ones at the landing place.

PREPARING TO REJOIN LOVED ONES

Souls in spirit remain very conscious of loved ones who are still incarnate. They are aware of how our lives unfold and connect with us whenever we think of them. These are *active* relationships that continue through all the years of separation. As death approaches, take time to remember all the souls you love who are in spirit. Enjoy sweet reminiscence; nourish yourself with images that promote fondness and affection. Such feelings of love can:

- ✦ Call these souls to you in reassuring predeath visits.
- ✦ Call these particular souls to be present as you arrive in the landing place.
- ✦ Attune your soul to recognize and receive "sensations" of love in the afterlife. As mentioned before, this attunement helps direct your attention to the presence of love (guides and soul friends) in the landing place. Further, it helps protect you from fear-based hallucinations or imaginings born of old religious beliefs.

THE DARK DOOR

Death appears to us as a dark door. Beyond the door is a secret that we yearn for and often fear. The amnesia we were born with—so we would take this life and its lessons seriously—keeps the dark door tightly shut and fuels our imaginings of the other side.

While death is a minor event for a soul, a mere transition ushering us toward the afterlife, it offers one significant challenge. Our soul knowledge—remembering past lives, our soul group, and all the wisdom acquired in our incarnations—doesn't spontaneously reappear after death. The exception is more advanced souls who've grown and evolved over many past lives. For most of us, though, the period immediately after death can be confusing because the amnesia fades slowly. In some cases where souls don't know they've died, where they have great fear or retain an intense attachment to their physical life, or where they have lived selfish lives devoid of love, the amnesia may endure for a long period.

This is the precise reason for this book and the ancient books of the dead. In many cases, souls require a significant revivification period to remember who they are. All this explains why the transitional bardos exist—to offer an extended period for the soul to remember its essence, its purpose, and its history.

Reuniting hastens and advances the process of remembering who we are. Many souls, on first glimpsing a lost loved one, are still far from aware of their place in spirit. All they know is that someone who abandoned them in death has returned. The joy is great, but confusion and amnesia may yet continue.

The surge of love ignited by reuniting often starts the awakening of our soul knowledge. Bits and pieces of shared past lives can begin to show up. There is a returning sense of belonging—first to our group and finally to the *whole*. The dark door begins to open, and we commence to grasp who we've been and where we are going now.

SOUL GROWTH

As we reunite—first at the landing place with guides and loved ones and later in our group—there is something we must face. We have changed. The returning soul has altered energy and new wisdom from the just-completed life. And the welcoming souls have changed as well by virtue of their own incarnations. Every visit to Earth (or our chosen planet) is a long, arduous journey that alters us in profound ways.

As we return to the *whole*, to *all*, we bring back new knowledge, but we also bring back our own transformed self. While our soul essence remains, in some ways we are new. It's much like college friends who've lived apart for years in different countries meeting again. So much life has been lived in the intervening years, and there have been so many losses, joys, and struggles, that the old friendship must go through a readjustment. At first, they bask in old memories. But then they must catch up and delicately seek to recognize how each has changed. This is the same process that souls go through while reuniting in the afterlife. They must carefully, and with love, recalibrate a new sense of each other. This process of discovery can be very intimate and beautiful. But it can also be jarring because a single lifetime may carve in us great change.

HOME

In this book of the dead, you have a star map, a navigation guide to the afterlife. It is meant to help you through the transition and some of the important moments of discarnate life. It can also be used to protect you from fear. Remember— you will be received, you will be cared for, and you will be loved. That is the absolute truth about the time after death. And it's the core of what you need to know.

That said, developing your own navigational skills now is a tremendous asset in the immediate postdeath afterlife. Books of the dead—and this is no exception—are the original self-help guides. While many of the ancient books are more myth than truth, they all offered skills to find landmarks in the afterlife terrain.

Welcome to your death, to this journey. It is one I have taken many times. I hold up the lamp for you to see ahead, to help you walk unafraid. We, on the other side, wish you bon voyage as you let go of this life. We are waiting for you, and we will welcome you home. I promise you that the dark door will open and that the light of love will take you in.

How to Channel

CHANNELING DATES BACK TO PRIMITIVE, preliterate cultures. The shaman was the designated intermediary between a particular tribe and the spirit realm. Through chanting, dancing, sleep deprivation, fasting, hyperventilation, or psychoactive plants, the shaman entered an altered state that opened the channel to entities on the other side who, in turn, would offer coded information and help.

The Egyptian Book of the Dead was channeled by priests using "essential statues" that focused attention and put them into trance states. Channeling is also the likely source of *The Tibetan Book of the Dead* (oracles would open themselves to be temporarily possessed by spirits who would then teach and offer prophecies), and the Vedas (Hindu sacred texts).

The Greek Dionysian cults (sixth century BCE) used wine and plant-based drugs to create altered states and channel spirit guides called *Angelos*—or messengers. They also used *psychomanteums*—mirrors—for connecting to the spirit world.

Much of the Bible is channeled. Yahweh channeled through his chosen Moses, David, Solomon, Samuel, Daniel, Elijah, Ezekiel, Jeremiah, Isaiah and John the Baptist all received channeled messages. St. John's book of Revelation is channeled as well. Zoroaster, in the Arab world, created the Avesta text that included channeled guidance regarding moral laws and the nature of the spirit world. The Qur'an derives from channeled visionary material when Muhammad experienced a Divine presence—Allah.

The history of religion can generally be understood as the history of channeling. In fact, Jon Klimo suggests that, "Channeling includes most major recorded spiritual communication between physical and non-physical beings."*

In the modern era, channels such as Edgar Cayce, Alice Bailey (the Tibetan), Ruth Montgomery, Jane Roberts (Seth), Helen Cohn Schucman (*A Course in Miracles*), J. Z. Knight (Ramtha), and Kevin Ryerson have vastly increased our knowledge of the spirit world and why we incarnate on this planet. These modern channels universally agree on the following:

+ God is us and we are God. We are not separate from God but all part of the Divine. The universal collective consciousness—*all that is*—is not a figure with a white beard but the entirety of all souls, all consciousness together.
+ Souls incarnate again and again. We do not live just once.
+ While there are bardos where souls adjust to being dead and heal from pain and confusion in their lives, there is no hell. There is no prince of darkness tempting us into damnation. There is no punishment.
+ We come to Earth to learn and evolve as individual souls and ultimately bring back what we've learned to *all that is*—God.
+ We are all one while also retaining our own soul identity.

CHANNELING FOR EVERYONE

Channeling is not the exclusive province of mystics, prophets, seers, or mediums. It requires no special gifts of clairaudience, no access to spiritual visions, no ordination into a mystery school or any form

---

*Jon Klimo, *Channeling* (Berkeley, Calif.: North Atlantic Books, 1998).

of priesthood. Channeling is like prayer—anyone can do it. *You* can do it if you care to follow the simple steps of the process and begin a two-way communication to entities in spirit. They are a thought away. The mere *intention* to communicate opens the channel.

Steps to the Channeling Process

1. Select a place to channel that supports feeling safe and grounded. It could be at a solid-feeling desk or table or in a chair that you associate with comfort and calm.

2. Decide on a spiritual address to send your questions and messages. Is there a particular loved soul, now in the afterlife, with whom you want to communicate? Do you want to send questions to your spirit guide, the one who supports and watches over you? Another choice would be to send questions and messages to the part of your own soul that always remains in spirit—to communicate with your higher self, your own soul knowledge. You might also choose to communicate with the Divine/the whole/ *all that is*/God. Before attempting to channel, be clear which entity you are seeking to reach.

3. Select a talisman—an object that represents your connection to the entity you'll channel. If it's someone you loved on Earth who is now in spirit, you might use an object that belonged to them or that they gave to you. Otherwise choose a talisman that symbolizes your spirit guide, higher self, or God—whichever you plan to channel. Mandalas, sacred stones, crystals, Buddhist or Celtic knots, and other symbols of spirit are often used.

4. Use an object—candles work well—for eye fixation. If you choose a candle flame for your focus, find a base that's pleasing in a color you associate with peace, nature, or spiritual connection. Always use the same base—the accoutrements of ritual are important.

5. Take a breath, and as you slowly exhale, feel the *intention* to make contact, to open the channel.

6. Begin a mindful breath meditation. This meditation creates a mild altered state—a doorway to the other side.

   • Focus awareness on the diaphragm—the genesis and center of your breath. Breathe in and out slowly.

   • On your first out-breath, count *one;* with your second out-breath count *two,* and so on until you reach *ten.* Repeat for one or two more cycles of ten breaths, or until you feel significantly relaxed and receptive.

   • When a thought arises, notice but don't dwell on the thought. Return your attention as soon as possible to your breath. Thoughts will always show up during meditation; this is normal and should never be judged as some sort of failure. Your only task is to return awareness to your breath each time you notice a thought.

   • Keep watching the candle flame throughout your meditation.

7. Use a light divination to expand openness and receptivity by imagining a star of light about six inches above your head. It is a reflection of the candle flame before you. Now visualize the star expanding until it is an orb of yellow light—the color of the sun. This light above you is the channel, the connecting place between you and those in the spirit world (your loved ones, spirit guides, your own soul in spirit, or God). The channel is now open. And your mere *intention* to connect keeps it so.

8. Keep a record of every channeled conversation. You will find it important to review this over time, as there will be much wisdom in your journal. In a special notebook that you keep only for channeling, physically write your first question. Maintain openness to whatever you receive in response to your question.

9. Watch the words form on the page. The answer will show up in a variety of ways. Usually, in the beginning, the communication is halting. A word or two will come. Just write them down without judging or trying to understand what they mean. Listen to the voice in your mind. After the first word or two, wait. Stay open to receive the next phrase or the rest of the sentence—and write that down too. Wait again—there may be more.

Note that the communications you receive can take other forms; especially as you get more practiced at channeling. These alternate forms can include:

- The download. These are complete and complex ideas that *you* have to find words to describe. The communication comes only as a picture, a diagram, or a concept.
- The rush. This is a series of words and sentences that come rapid-fire—often faster than you can write.
- The telescoped answer. Often this can be one or two potent words, such as "all love ... stay ... always ... with you," and so on.

10. When there is a period of silence and the communication has apparently stopped, write down your next question. Continue this process until needing to rest or sensing that you've done enough. Because channeled answers, particularly at the beginning, are often so brief, you might consider asking simple yes-or-no questions at the start.

11. Accept the inevitable doubts and judgments that arise. There is no way to have certainty that the voice in your mind is the soul or guide or divinity you've addressed. And you will periodically have doubt or fear that channeling is a form of self-deception. Keep channeling in the face of these thoughts—everyone has them. If you persevere, you will acquire—over time—a written body of love, wisdom, and deep knowledge. It will move you; it will support you; it will guide you.

Things You Can Ask via Channeling

+ Try simple yes-or-no questions at the beginning—"Are you happy?" for example.
+ Ask questions, if you're interested, about the soul's transition.
+ Ask for advice or support.
+ Ask about the nature of the afterlife.
+ Ask about your life purpose, your direction.
+ Ask for wisdom to make good choices.
+ Ask how best to love and how to act on love in daily life.
+ Ask for or offer forgiveness.
+ Ask for help facing difficult things, painful emotions, or destructive desires/impulses.

Things Not to Ask for While Channeling

+ The future is off limits in channeling. Entities from the spirit world are not allowed to reveal the future because such knowledge prevents you from learning and making decisions of free will.
+ Entities from the other side, with rare exceptions, cannot fix things. What they CAN do is support you to make the wisest choices as you face challenging situations. Don't ask for intercessions, for the course of events to change, or for help unraveling problems.
+ Medical intercessions are beyond the allowed capabilities of discarnate souls or guides. Asking for medical cures or changes in prognosis can result in channel blockage. The souls on the other side can't give this to you, and your determination to get help may prevent you from hearing their response.
+ Entities from spirit can't change the behavior of others. They can't get a child to stop self-destructive patterns, make a landlord

say "yes" if you need a place to live, push a potential employer to give you a job, or help your team win the Super Bowl.

✦ Pain relief isn't a role for discarnate souls or spirit guides. Don't ask entities on the other side to take away suffering or protect you from painful experiences on Earth. They will help you *face* pain, but not avoid it.

CHANNELING AS A HEALING TOOL AND ITS IMPACT ON GRIEF

Channeling is about listening and connecting to spirit. The pain we struggle with in our incarnate lives can be seen through a different lens when we channel. This pain, born of all our emotional and physical struggles, is about growing and learning.

Channeling can provide the relief of knowing that the soul of your loved one survives. That soul is happy, surrounded by love, and the painful circumstances of their death are over. Channeling allows you to offer and receive forgiveness for mistakes and to realize they are now unimportant.

Through channeling, you can learn that your loved one lives in a community of souls. The deep love between these souls is eternal and cannot be affected by death. Conversely, your relationship to your loved one is unbroken and will continue for all time.

If the loss of your loved one was traumatic, you can also learn why or how it happened, including how it fits with your life purpose and lesson plan for this incarnation. You can receive help and wisdom for what to do now and how to rebuild your life around this purpose and mission.

Remember, your loved one is just a thought away, and you can connect virtually at will.

Channeling offers an opportunity to know where we come from and where we are going. So often we feel lost, trying to make sense of what has been taken from us and why we experience so much struggle. The answers come from listening to the other side. We are not alone here; we are loved and supported.

Matthew's Experience of Death through Past Life Regression

THERE IS ONLY ONE WAY to experience death and the afterlife while still living and that is through a special form of hypnotic regression. Over the past twenty years, hypnosis has been used to open the door to past lives. With Michael Newton's 1994 discovery of the life between lives induction and similar trance-inducing processes, hypnosis can also be used to observe the moment of death and peer into our existence in the spirit world.*

After Jordan died, I wanted to break the glass that separated my existence as Matthew from the soul knowledge that could shine light on why I'm here, what death is, and what lies beyond. I also felt the strongest urge to know where Jordan was and learn more about how we were connected beyond the father-son relationship we had in this life. To do this, I sought the services of Ralph Metzner, Ph.D., a psychologist who specializes in past life regressions and after-death communication. While Metzner facilitated my journeys to many past lives, in only one instance did I get to see the life-between-lives and learn about key landmarks in the spirit world. This is the story of that regression.

Metzner is a frail man, shrunken into his chair. He was once a mountain climber, an athlete, but he now moves with a tentative grace. A master

---

*Michael Newton, *Journey of Souls* (Woodbury, Minn.: Llewellyn Publications, 1994).

of inducing trance, he asks me to visualize orbs of light—above my head, above my heart, and above my pelvis—and to let them carry me away from the familiar objects of my life toward a channel opening to spirit. I'm encouraged to cross the border to a place where I can feel my own soul knowledge, where I have access to memories of past lives and the existence between them. Within a few minutes, I have entered the eighteenth century, where I was a bookbinder, and Jordan was my wife.

In that incarnation, Jordan died young, exposing me to enormous grief and disconnection. As that life ended, I was an old man, living in a sparsely furnished room, with just my memories and a stack of scientific books that I had bound. Most were in Latin, and I was unable even to read them. I had been frail and sick for a long time, shuffling from window to bed, craving the light of day, yet feeling myself drift further and further from the affairs of my life. Dying of pneumonia, with only a neighbor woman to minister to me, I began to slip out of my body. Once I had, the pain in my lungs immediately ceased, and I watched as my neighbor closed my eyes and pulled the blanket over my head.

I felt detached, suspended above the scene. I looked at the objects of my room: the fireplace and pot for cooking, the pile of books of which I'd been so proud, my thin straw mattress. Grief consumed me—not so much because of my aloneness, but because of how I'd let go of love, of connection. When my wife (Jordan) died, I had simply retreated into a walled place inside, which loss couldn't reach.

I found myself backing to the window. The stacked leather volumes and their gilt-embossed titles seemed less important now. My body lay distant and still in the dark interior of the room. I slipped through the wall and saw that the street below was bathed in sunlight. A horse restlessly pulled at its traces as I moved higher without any effort. Without willing it, without direction or intention, I rose above the street. I watched, curious but strangely unafraid, as the familiar shapes of walls and buildings receded below me. In a few moments, I ascended through cloud cover, and all that was below me disappeared. The clouds morphed to a dull gray without discernible shape or texture. I felt unrooted from time and space, perhaps moving but with little expectation of what awaited me.

I was still struggling with a sense of failure from the last years of my life. Regret seemed to cover me like dust accumulated over a long journey. I could see in all directions, yet there wasn't the slightest variation in the monochromatic gray surrounding me. In time, there was more light. The gray above me held an intense luminosity. The light became sky, a deep cerulean blue, while below I could see some sort of solid ground. It was a path. On either side, I saw grass, flower beds, and low, blossoming bushes. The grass was an unnatural emerald color, and the flowers, though beautiful, were more radiantly colored than on Earth. I was in a garden. It stretched forward a great distance with no apparent boundaries.

I moved down the path without effort or choice and without actually walking. I noticed that I could see everything—in front of and behind me—360 degrees. A tall, robed soul, that I knew to be a guide, appeared. I told the guide that I found the garden peaceful but oddly disturbing with its glittering, over-bright colors and said this was not a place I knew. The guide told me telepathically that what I saw—the garden and path and sky—was here for my comfort, and I remember thinking it was too weird to be comforting. I was told the garden was made of energy, not matter, and that I could touch it, but how it felt (rubbing the grass, for example) would be the way I expected it to feel. More accurately, how I hallucinated it to feel.

As I moved down the path, the colors became more intense, almost throbbing. The tall guide was at my side, and it was as if we were going for a stroll. I was told I was safe, cared for. Love radiated from the guide. At that moment, my brother, who'd died before me in that life as the bookbinder, appeared. I was overjoyed. And as I gazed at *his countenance—so familiar in that life—I also knew him as my father in my current life. A woman appeared—my wife, Elzbeth, in the bookbinder's life. And then, almost instantly, I knew her as my son, Jordan. These beautiful souls, whom I love so much, held me and filled me with a happiness that exploded like an igniting sun. The emotions—of love, of gratitude—were bigger than I'd ever known, bigger than a human body could hold.*

The garden began to dissolve, and I was told that I was ready to enter the spirit world, but there was no gate or obvious transition. I found myself in a vast room where souls appeared bent in prayer or contemplation. There were no sounds. My wife and brother were gone now; I drifted to a spot where I settled and entered some kind of trance state. The first images I saw were of myself as a very young child in the seaside town where I grew up. I was crying.

Almost immediately, my perspective shifted, and I was watching myself from the outside as I bent in contemplation. I could no longer see the images of my life review yet, strangely, I could feel emotions that were being triggered by whatever I saw. My soul was filled at various moments with empathic pain, sweet filigrees of affection, surges of love, and profound loss and regret. The emotions were intense and pure, beautiful and painful, and devoid of defensiveness, judgment, or anger. They were simply my reactions to seeing the truth of that life.

To my tremendous relief, the ordeal of life review ended. My guide told me that we were about to visit my council of elders. There was some kind of transition, which I don't recall, and I found myself in a domed chamber. What seemed like filtered sunlight came in through the dome. Members of my council were in front of me, wearing robes of various colors. Some of these souls appeared quite large, while others were relatively diminutive. Most of them were familiar from conferences following other lives. The council conveyed telepathically (it was hard to distinguish individual communications) that I had given great love to Elzbeth and my children. There were comments on the strength and integrity of that love. But then the council examined how I had withdrawn from relationship and love in the face of pain and loss. The bookbinder closed himself up and built the remainder of his life on small pleasures and routines. I was shown how this pattern of disconnection extended from other past lives and had yet to be overcome. My next incarnation would require working on this same lesson.

After the council review, I was taken to my soul group (again I don't remember how). The feeling was one of coming home—to where I was safe and loved—after a long absence.

I joined my soul group in a meadow of high grass surrounded by tall trees. A fallen tree pierced the meadow diagonally, and along that trunk—standing, leaning, sitting on the log or in the grass—was my group. There was a sweet, beautiful feeling of sinking into their midst. I was greeted—sometimes singly, sometimes held by a small group. The meadow, while just a welcoming scene created of energy, filled me with peace. I had the sense that this web of love had always held me, will always hold me.

Some of the souls were still incarnate and a bit paler than the rest. Some were fully in spirit—vibrant, showing all their love and acquired wisdom. We have all gone to Earth together many times. Not like soldiers to battle but as students to a most difficult school. There, our bodies and minds have borne scars, and we have learned from every one of them. But at this moment I was home. For a while. Soon I would embark on a different form of learning—where souls extract knowledge from their own histories and acquire skills they'll use to serve others in the spirit world. But now, in the meadow, all that could wait.

Afterword

Cassandra Vieten, Ph.D.

IN MY CAREER AS SOMEONE who studies extraordinary experiences and their transformative effects on people's lives, I've encountered thousands of awe-inspiring, goose-bump-inducing, heart-opening, mind-blowing, profoundly moving, out-of-this-world reports.

Matthew McKay's book, written by his deceased son, Jordan, and channeled through Matthew, is an exemplar of how perceptions beyond the ordinary can change our entire worldview and perspective. Our studies on transformations in worldview at the Institute of Noetic Sciences (IONS) show that once a person has had a transformation that is fully embodied and integrated—a shift to consciousness that takes hold at the roots—people like Matthew are compelled to share their insights to ease suffering and promote well-being of others. Like the Return in Joseph Campbell's Hero's Journey, the transformational process is not complete until the hero brings back the boon—the gifts, clarity, and insights he or she has obtained during the journey—to share with the community at large.

In this book, Matthew, through deep exploration of his relationship with his son, Jordan (pre- and postdeath), has endeavored to provide perhaps one of the greatest boons that could be imagined—a road map to ease the minds of future intrepid travelers, an antidote to the fear of what lies beyond the veil. This journey into the unknown requires enormous courage, and this book is a gift beyond measure. From its final chapter (p. 103):

> In this book of the dead, you have a star map, a navigation guide to the afterlife. It is meant to help you through the transition and some of the important moments of discarnate life. It can also be used to protect you from fear. Remember—you will be received, you will be cared for, and you will be loved. That is the absolute truth about the time after death. And it's the core of what you need to know.
>
> That said, developing your own navigational skills now is a tremendous asset in the immediate postdeath afterlife. Books of the dead—and this is no exception—are the original self-help guides. While many of the ancient books are more myth than truth, they all offered skills to find landmarks in the afterlife terrain.

I can't help but feel that this book is at once a love letter from Jordan to his father, a love letter from Jordan through his father to humanity as a whole, and a love letter from Matthew to Jordan and his once and future self.

At this point, a skeptical reader might ask me, a psychologist and a scientist (albeit with some fairly unconventional interests): Was this real? Imagined? Confabulated? The only way that a father who had experienced the unimaginable could cope? Or could it be veridical?

My honest answer is threefold.

First, it's impossible to say for certain whether this case study is "real" in the materialist sense of the word. It could be completely real in this sense, and this beautiful and wise guide could speak of an actual (not metaphorical or symbolic) and very real state and place of being that we all come from and will return to. Thousands of recorded accounts of the afterlife speak of this place—from details of near-death experiences, to reports from those purporting to be channels or mediums, narratives of millions of people's personal subjective experiences, and the sacred texts and teachings of most of the world's religious, spiritual, and indigenous traditions. Though too complicated for this short afterword, there is also the possibility (indeed, likelihood) that our current epistemology (how we know things) and ontology (what we know) of "reality" is limited and essentially flawed. There may be places and things that cannot be measured, predicted, or manipulated, yet are very real nonetheless.*

Second, there is some scholarly theory and research on the possibility of survival of consciousness after bodily death,† though empirical studies are scant. Given the enormous implications, it's hard to believe that this is not one of the most funded research topics in history! In addition, there is very little research on the phenomenon of channeling, even though reports abound of people feeling like they are "receiving" information from outside of themselves. The divide between the natural sciences and the investigation of subjective experience, and the fear of contaminating science with metaphysics (as though science were a fragile and fainting thing that could not withstand rigorous investigation of what are clearly naturally occurring perceptions if not full-blown phenomena), has kept this from being the case. Even Thomas Edison said, "People say I have created things. I have never created anything. I get impressions from the Universe at large and work them out, but I am only a plate on a record or a

---

*Edward F. Kelly, Adam Crabtree, and Paul Marshall, eds., *Beyond Physicalism: Toward Reconciliation of Science and Spirituality* (Lanham, Md.: Rowman & Littlefield, 2015); Edward F. Kelly, Emily Williams Kelly, Adam Crabtree, Alan Gauld, Michael Grosso, and Bruce Greyson, *Irreducible Mind: Toward a Psychology or the 21st Century* (Lanham, Md.: Rowman & Littlefield, 2009).
†See the website of the Department of Perceptual Studies at the University of Virginia, the Windbridge Research Institute website, Peter Fenwick's work, and the website of the Institute of Noetic Sciences. Also see the more community-based Eternea website and the International Association for Near Death Studies (IANDS) website.

receiving apparatus—what you will. Thoughts are really impressions that we get from outside."* It's time for us to support rigorous scientific investigation into these questions to deepen our understanding of who we are and the nature of reality, to potentially reduce fear, grief, and suffering, and to enhance thriving.

Third, whether or not it is "real" is the wrong question. The question is, What wisdom can we gain from this exploration? How can these practices of channeling, contemplation, and listening be helpful to us in this life and in preparing for and navigating death? I found that multiple truths about living, from the perspective of the deceased, emerge in each chapter, such as the difference between pain and despair (p. 27):

> Souls who despair have missed the point of life. They think life is about achieving happiness and that pain indicates a blatant failure. But life isn't about being happy. It's about learning to love, no matter what level of pain or suffering we face. The pain is an essential part of the lesson, not a sign of failure.
>
> Despair is really the inability to express and act on love during periods of extended pain.

The voice of Jordan describing his fellow travelers also feels quite genuine and rings true in a pragmatic way, such as on page 44:

> We aren't playing harps, sitting on clouds, or drinking grog in some Viking Valhalla. We aren't living in mansions or walking in sandaled feet on the courtyards of temples. We are just a group of souls who learn and love together.

---

*Thomas Alva Edison quoted in Neil Baldwin, *Edison: Inventing the Century* (New York: Hyperion, 1995), 376.

Other aspects of the death experience reminded me of the people I've studied who practice nonduality or have experienced nondual awakening. The earlier mentioned studies of transformative experiences at the Institute of Noetic Sciences find their roots in the experience of our founder, Apollo 14 astronaut Edgar Mitchell, who had such a profound experience of interconnectedness on his way back from his moonwalk that he spent the remainder of his life working to understand and disseminate the potential of oneness globally. In Jordan's voice, this "merger with the whole" is one of the soul's primary tasks. On page 60, he tells us:

> It is like walking into a forest and suddenly *being* the forest. It's like lying on a beach and at once becoming the sand, the waves, and the sky. . . . Merging with the whole is knowing the truth of things, the beauty of things. And that knowing creates an energy—a vibrational force—that is the deepest form of connection and love.

From such a place, why would anyone want to return? Or as Joseph Campbell put it: "The first problem of the returning hero is to accept as real, after an experience of the soul-satisfying vision of fulfillment, the passing joys and sorrows, banalities and noisy obscenities of life. Why re-enter such a world?"* For this, Jordan notes that discarnate souls do miss things that go along with having bodies, such as eating, sex, and touch, and that these things, along with the drive to learn and grow, make it worth deciding to embark on another incarnation. But more subtly (from p. 93),

---

*Joseph Campbell, *The Hero with a Thousand Faces* (Novato, Calif.: New World Library, 2008, 3rd ed.), 189.

Souls remember the beauty of loss, the light of the imperfect, and all that was learned colliding against the hard edges of life. So the planet where we incarnate is like an oft-visited foreign country that we remember with love and yearn to see once more.

The experience Jordan shares offers a poetic and pragmatic map for what may happen when we die, and it is a deft guide for living this life as well.

CASSANDRA VIETEN, PH.D., is the executive director of the John W. Brick Mental Health Foundation, scholar-in-residence at the Arthur C. Clarke Center for Human Imagination at the University of California, San Diego, and senior fellow at the Institute of Noetic Sciences, where she was president from 2013–2019. She is a psychologist, mind-body medicine researcher, author of numerous articles in scientific journals, and an internationally recognized keynote speaker.

Index